AMERICA'S CUP

including the
Louis Vuitton Cup

2000

PAUL LARSEN & RUSSELL COUTTS

Principal Photography DANIEL FORSTER

Hodder Moa Beckett

Acknowledgements

The authors give special thanks and sincere appreciation to Carlton J. Pinheiro, Curator of the Herreshoff Marine Museum and the America's Cup Hall of Fame. Mr Pinheiro made an exhaustive search of the museum's archives to locate many rare photographs, some never before published, to help illustrate the history of this unique sporting event.

Photographer Paul Darling also deserves special mention for his contribution of images of the early 12-metre races, including what is believed to be the first colour photograph ever taken of America's Cup action. And the photographic record included in this book would not have been possible without the work of Daniel Forster, Dan Nerney and Christian Fevrier.

We also owe a large debt to the many America's Cup writers and historians who came before us, especially: John Rousmaniere, Stanley Rosenfeld, Roger Vaughan, John Bertrand, Bob Fisher, Michael Levitt, Barbara Lloyd, Thomas Lawson, Winfield M. Thompson, Dennis Conner, Bob Bavier, Bruce Stannard, Ivor Wilkins, and Doug Riggs.

An undertaking such as this would not have been possible without the help of many. Thanks to Sarah Beresford who got the project going, Kevin Chapman who kept it going, Janette Howe, Nick Turzynski and the outstanding professionals at Hodder Moa Beckett who made it happen.

Many other friends and colleagues lent a hand, including: Scott MacLeod, Gay Larsen, Peter Scott, Kristen Sneyd, Jamie France, Nick Holroyd, Tom Schnackenberg, D. J. Cathcart and Peter Montgomery.

Russell Coutts
Paul Larsen
August 25, 1999

Picture Credits — Unless otherwise stated, all images are copyright Daniel Forster.

Carlo Borlenghi: 119, 121.

Paul Darling: 54, 55, 56 (right), 57 (right), 60 (right), 82.

Fast 2000: 132.

Christian Fevrier: 7, 8-9, 12-13, 27, 28-29, 34 (bottom left and middle right), 38-39, 46 (left), 67 (right), 73 (bottom right), 79 (top right and bottom right), 94 (bottom), 99 (bottom left), 117, 129, 130, 175 (bottom left), 179 (bottom left), 182 (bottom left), 185 (top right).

AmericaOne, Sharon Green: 115, 141, 142.

Bob Grieser: 155, 161 (top right).

Mike Harvey: 150.

Herreshoff Marine Museum: 46 (centre (Nicholas Whitman and N. Bonnington collection) and right), 47, 48 (left (Charlotte Young collection) and right), 49 (left and right(Du Wolf collection)), 50-51 (J.P. Brightman collection), 51 (Edwin Levick collection), 52, 53, 81, 172 (left (Bachrach collection), centre and right).

Aloha Racing, Sheila Hill: 138, 139 (middle and right).

Imageworks: 11.

Fay Looney: 32-33.

Nico Martinez: 127.

Dan Nerney: 23 (top right), 34 (top left and middle left), 56 (left), 57 (left), 58, 59, 61, 62 (left), 76-77, 79 (top left), 89 (top left, middle right and bottom right), 91 (inset), 125 (top right), 131 (top left), 133 (top), 135, 137 (bottom left and centre), 146 (bottom left), 149, 151 (top), 154 (top left), 185 (bottom right).

New Zealand Herald: 17 (top right and middle right), 42, 109 (top).

New Zealand Tourism Board: 37 (inset), 42.

G. Martin Raget: 131 (bottom left).

Skyworks: 41 (top, middle left, middle right and bottom right).

Kaoru Soehata, Photowave Ltd.: 123, 124, 125 (bottom left and bottom right), 158, 162, 170-171, 178.

Stars & Stripes: 151 (Barbara Martin Photography).

Team New Zealand: 74-75, 99 (top left and bottom right), 100-101 (Rob Tucker), 103, 107 (Rob Tucker), 108, 109 (bottom left, bottom centre and bottom right), 156-157, 175 (bottom right), 179 (bottom right), 185 (centre).

Ivor Wilkins: Endpapers, 5, 6, 96-97, 100-101, 107, 111.

Young America, Jane Eagleson: 153.

America True, Tom Zinn: 147.

ISBN 1-86958-717-0

© 1999 – Original text by Russell Coutts and Paul Larsen
The moral rights of the authors have been asserted

© 1999 Design and format – Hodder Moa Beckett Publishers Limited

Published in 1999 by Hodder Moa Beckett Publishers Limited, [a member of the Hodder Headline Group]; 4 Whetu Place, Mairangi Bay, Auckland, New Zealand

Produced and designed by Hodder Moa Beckett Publishers Ltd
Film by Microdot, Auckland
Printed by Toppan Printing Co, Hong Kong

AMERICA'S CUP

2000

Foreword

By John Bertrand A.M.

For people who race sailboats and those who are fascinated by 80-foot yachts slicing through the ocean powered solely by the wind, the America's Cup represents the ultimate in the sport. In February 2000, two such boats will meet at the starting line in the waters off Auckland, New Zealand. They will race to determine temporary ownership of the world's oldest athletic trophy. On board one of the boats will be sixteen crewmen representing Team New Zealand, defenders of the America's Cup. They earned this honour by virtue of victory in the 29th edition of the races. At the helm was Russell Coutts, co-author of this book, who will once again be behind the wheel in the 30th America's Cup.

Who will be Team New Zealand's opponent has been the subject of an international guessing game ever since Coutts and crew sailed *Black Magic* over the finish line on May 13, 1995. At this writing it appears that thirteen challengers from six nations will begin their quest in October 1999 for the Louis Vuitton Cup and the right to meet the Kiwis in Cup competition.

As part of five Australian teams that have challenged to win the America's Cup in the past, I can readily testify to Messrs Coutts' and Larsen's comment that: "Personal sacrifice in the form of separation from family, friends and finances has customarily marked the quest". The modern event demands an almost all-consuming commitment to the endeavour, a fact well detailed in this book.

From my vantage point as skipper of *Australia II* and our now-historic America's Cup victory in 1983, I can confirm that the authors have captured much of what makes this event so unique. In their recounting of Cup history, their description of the testing and technology involved in producing state-of-the-art racing yachts, their analysis of the match racing format, and their profiles of many past and present America's Cup personalities, they have touched on why this single regatta has had such a magnetic attraction to sailors and spectators alike for almost a century and a half.

Following the victory of *Australia II* in 1983, the regatta moved in 1986/87 to Fremantle, Western Australia, where it enjoyed what many Cup followers believe was its most spectacular staging. New life was breathed into the old event by both the venue and the 13 challengers who hoped to return home with sailing's most prized trophy. Now that the regatta returns to the Southern Hemisphere, I believe that once again it will find new life and a whole new set of fans.

The Auckland America's Cup will feature a number of interesting contrasts. My old adversary Dennis Conner will return for his eighth America's Cup while teams from France and Australia are placing the emphasis on youth. Some teams will arrive in New Zealand with two new boats, some with one, and others with boats dating back to 1995 and even 1992. As pointed out in this book, designers working under the International America's Cup Class formula have to date created boats only for San Diego waters. The conditions in Auckland present a whole new set of challenges.

I am looking forward to the America's Cup with great anticipation and excitement.

John Bertrand A.M. was the skipper of Australia II *when he and his team pulled off one of the greatest upsets in modern sports history by winning the America's Cup in 1983, ending the 132-year winning streak achieved by the United States. He is now vice-chairman and co-founder of Quokka Sports Inc, the digital sports entertainment company which is providing the official internet coverage of the America's Cup at:*

www.americascup.org

Contents

Introduction
By Russell Coutts

One hundred and forty-eight years have passed since the yacht *America* won what was then called the 100 Guinea Cup. As I have researched the history of the Cup for this book, I have realised that although we may feel our developments and problems are new, often these were experienced more than a century ago. Professional crews, big budgets, battles fought through the media, and design and technology innovations have been part of the Cup since 1851. In many ways the traditions live on, repeating themselves time and again.

Many who experience Cup competition once can't stay away. Sir Thomas Lipton tried unsuccessfully five times and Syd Fischer has come to Auckland for his fifth attempt. Perhaps it is the sheer difficulty of the challenge that draws people back to the Cup almost like an addiction. Reputations have been made and, conversely, in some cases they have been destroyed. Yet if winning it was any easier, perhaps the event would die. For the team who win, it is their right to stage the event in their home country. For those that lose, it is almost a complete loss. Old boats become worthless to the point that they are almost a liability. In 1992, when New Zealand lost, it took me more than a year to stop thinking about it every night. After winning in 1995, it took me a year to stop celebrating!

New Zealand has only been a competitor in the Cup since 1986, with four unsuccessful attempts before winning it in 1995. It still seems almost unbelievable that 13 challengers will tow out to the starting line in October in the waters where many of the crew grew up and learnt how to sail what may well prove to be the best America's Cup event yet. I have no doubt looking at the challengers that this Cup will also be the toughest. New Zealand's changing conditions and strong winds should combine to make spectacular racing. The fight for the Louis Vuitton Cup to establish who will challenge Team New Zealand promises to be fascinating.

The answer is not always simple or predictable. This game is very difficult to win with sailing skills, fitness, design, financial backing, management and a good measure of luck all coming into play. In reality, it is often difficult to even compete in and get a challenge started. At least four teams who had originally entered have failed to make the starting line, including the British, who have been unable to mount a challenge since 1986.

Being able to recognise what is important and what is achievable in the time frame seems to be what this game is all about. Having the fastest boat usually is the critical advantage, but there are a few cases in the history of the Cup that you will read about in this book where this has not been the case. Crews pushing the limits, perhaps taking risks they normally wouldn't take in order to have a chance of winning. Designers eagerly waiting to see who has got the design puzzle most correct for 2000. Some may have been too conservative, while others will be guilty of pushing things beyond the limits. There have already been several broken masts in the lead-up and I would expect to see more.

In most America's Cups, one of the teams develops an advantage and new technology is discovered. It has been more than four years since the last race in 1995 and I can recall how surprised we were at the speed edge we had developed then. A slight improvement here and a slight tweak there and the performance gains added up to a significant advantage. The chance of seeing a development with new technology in 2000 is very probable if not an absolute certainty. However, on the other hand, I wouldn't be surprised to see two relatively even boats on the starting line to do battle for the 30th America's Cup.

With the new American Express New Zealand Cup Village and harbour, the celebrations during the turn of the millennium and with 13 challengers set to compete, this event promises much and will have been worth waiting for. New Zealanders will no doubt support the home team once a challenger is decided, but sailors and competing supporters will enjoy a great atmosphere where the New Zealand public will be knowledgeable about sailing. Television and internet coverage will be better than ever.

The challenger that faces Team New Zealand in 2000 will be very well prepared and ready to race, having competed in more than 70 qualification races. Team New Zealand will be towing out to that starting line for race one having not faced any outside opposition in any race with any real meaning. I have tried to picture what this will be like. I can only assume it will be different, just as it was in 1995 when we met the defender for the first time, not really knowing if their performance would contain surprises.

I cannot properly explain it but I am sure the whole crew felt differently about racing in the challenger finals versus the Cup match itself. I am sure that the atmosphere and pressure was something that all top yachtsmen would one day want to experience. The America's Cup is still the premier event in world sailing and it is definitely worth winning.

Personally, I have tasted both victory and defeat in Cup racing and I know which I prefer. Team New Zealand will definitely be putting their best effort forward and it will be with determination and a good healthy fear of losing in front of our home crowd that we will face the challenger in 2000. Let the racing begin!

The historic J-Boat Class which is still racing today. These magnificent boats will be seen in Auckland's waters during the 30th America's Cup. Pictured (from left) are *Endeavour*, *Shamrock* and *Velsheda*.

CHAPTER 1

From Plastic To Silver

F ew New Zealanders paid the America's Cup any attention before 1983. In other parts of the world, particularly the United States, it may have been viewed as the quintessential international yachting competition, but it had never made that impression on Kiwis. The event was more than a hundred years old before anyone in the Southern Hemisphere even participated in it.

For those in New Zealand who were interested in the sport of yachting, the Olympic Games was considered the ultimate challenge. And there was an understanding and appreciation that to get to the Olympics, sailors had to begin in small boats at a young age and work their way through dozens of regattas.

Sailing began to create heroes and generate increasing interest at the end of the 1950s and in the early '60s. When two New Zealanders, Peter Mander and Jack Cropp, brought home a gold medal from the 1956 Olympics, sailing began its ascendancy as one of the most popular sports in the country. Youth sailing programmes at clubs and schools were formed. The more experienced sailors competed in regattas held around the world and when Chris Bouzaid won the One Ton Cup in 1969, Kiwis realised their sailors had reached world-class status.

The late '70s proved the effectiveness of the earlier youth sailing programmes. Barry Thom was runner-up in the 1976 Laser World Championships and a year later finished second in the OK Dinghy Worlds held in Auckland. Peter Lester won the event that year and Clive Roberts had won it two years earlier when England hosted the regatta. Chris Dickson and Hamish Wilcox won the double-handed title at the World Youth Championships in 1978.

While New Zealand developed its sailing programmes, Australia was focusing its yacht racing efforts on the America's Cup. After the *Gretel* challenge in 1962, Australia returned to Newport, Rhode Island, then the venue of Cup competition, in '67, '70, '74, '77 and '80. In those five matches against the New York Yacht Club's defender, all raced in 12-metre boats, the Aussies' record was 2-20. New Zealanders were aware of these contests, but no serious thought was given to joining the fray.

All that changed in 1983 when the Australians arrived in the US with a fast boat atop a winged keel and an absolute determination to capture the America's Cup. How that single act electrified the victor's nation and brought both pride and dollars flowing Down Under did not go unnoticed across the Tasman. All of a sudden there was an "If they can do it, why can't we?" attitude that was whispered about in yacht clubs and corporate boardrooms. And the more the question was asked, the more the answer was "We can".

In many yachting circles throughout the world there is the common notion that Sir Michael Fay initiated the original challenge idea and championed it until it became a reality. Yet, according to Fay, the man who actually launched New Zealand into America's Cup orbit was a Belgian futures and commodities trader named Marcel Fachler. Based in Sydney, Fachler was an eye witness to Australia's extravagant reaction to winning the Cup and apparently believed his own business interests would be well served if he entered a challenge through the Royal New Zealand Yacht Squadron for the 1986/87 America's Cup.

Fachler's challenge took the yachting world by surprise, particularly the Royal New Zealand Yacht Squadron. It seems the Belgian neglected to officially advise the Squadron of his plans and the Kiwi yachtsmen discovered their involvement only by reading the morning newspaper. What followed were several days of member asking member: "Did you make the challenge?"

After Fachler submitted both the challenge and the initial money to make it official, he suffered a string of business reversals and effectively disappeared. But by then, the idea of a real challenge had excited too many to disappear with him. This was uncharted territory, however, and for a while it appeared likely that the challenge would fold. Then yacht designer Ron Holland and yachting journalist Alan Sefton identified the young merchant bankers Michael Fay and partner David Richwhite as two people with the financial grunt, the organisational skills and, not least, the vision to take up the challenge.

Fay, then the 37-year-old managing partner of the merchant banking firm Fay Richwhite & Company in Auckland, took the request under advisement. He organised a number of what he called "think tank" sessions with the elite of New Zealand's yachting community.

"The think tank sessions provided positive answers for all four major issues. Yes, we had the design talent, the construction expertise, the sailors, and, with effort, we could find the money. On the design question, the names that kept coming up in addition to Ron Holland were Laurie Davidson and Bruce Farr. So I came up with the design team idea. What I said to Aussie Malcolm was, it's your job to go and put a design group together and I think three heads are going to be better than one on this project.... So the actual design group was put together by Aussie Malcolm."[1]

Fay put together a plan that included two critical decisions that had significant impact on the entire campaign. The first was to build identical boats out of fibreglass and the second was to enter the 12-metre World Championships to be held in Fremantle, Australia, in February 1986.

If the decision to enter New Zealand as a challenger was a surprise, the fibreglass idea was met with astonishment. Since 1958 when 12-metre yachts were first used in the America's Cup, every defender and challenger had built racers out of either wood or aluminium. Other designers had considered fibreglass, but it was rejected because it is costly and cannot be reshaped, cut, or welded like aluminium. Yet it offers several features that the Kiwis recognised as critical to their efforts. A fibreglass boat requires less fairing and can be made lighter than a boat of the same size built of aluminium. But the real genius of the idea was that two boats made from the same fibreglass mould at the same time would create two identical boats and they would be less expensive to produce than two aluminium boats built at different times.

[1] *Course to Victory*, Larsen and Coutts, Hodder Moa Beckett, 1995.

Sir Michael Fay was the man behind the early New Zealand challenges.

Laurie Davidson, Ron Holland, Bruce Farr and Russell Bowler (from left to right) made up the design team for the first New Zealand challenge. They sit in the first fibreglass 12-metre yacht ever built.

Gold medal winners in the 1956 Olympics, Jack Cropp (left) and Peter Mander (centre), who alerted the world to New Zealand's sailing prowess. Pictured here with manager and reserve J. E. Gillingham.

KZ-7 with a damaged mainsail after race five. The mainsail was not able to be lowered, threatening to break the mast. Earle Williams was sent aloft to cut the mainsail down. He was forced to free climb the top section of the mast because no halyard was available to hoist him.

A broken mast on KZ-3, New Zealand's first fibreglass 12-metre.

New Zealand introduced fibreglass into the boatbuilding equation in the country's first attempt to win the America's Cup in 1986/87. The "Plastic Fantastics" took the Cup world by storm and almost pulled off an unbelievable victory before falling to Dennis Conner and crew.

By using two identical boats to test sails, keels, rudders, and even entire teams, the Kiwis knew immediately what worked and what didn't. Two-boat programmes had been used in the past but because the boats were never identical there were greater difficulties in validating whether what was being tested made the difference or whether the difference was inherent in the designs of the two boats. Producing identical boats was one of the most significant design advancements in modern America's Cup history and one that would pay enormous dividends for New Zealand just nine years later.

Once the challenge was assured of continuing, the designers started work and the building material was determined, then it was time to settle on who would sail the boats. Only a handful of Kiwis had ever been on a 12-metre yacht as was used in America's Cup competition at the time. One of those was Chris Dickson.

Although just 23 years old in 1985, Dickson had earned a reputation as one of New Zealand's top sailors after outstanding performances in national, world and Olympic competitions. And in addition to big boat experience, he was adept at match racing, the one-on-one racing format used in the America's Cup. He was selected to skipper the first New Zealand challenge.

By the time the 12-metre World Championship was held in Fremantle in February 1986, the first two of three fibreglass boats were built. Given the official registration designations of *KZ-3* and *KZ-5*, both were entered in the regatta. Dickson was at the helm of *KZ-5* and Graeme Woodroffe steered her stablemate. In truth, few expected either boat to do very well as neither the syndicate nor the sailors had any experience in this type of regatta. When the final scores were posted and Chris Dickson aboard *KZ-5* was listed in second place behind *Australia III*, eyebrows met hairlines throughout the world of sailboat racing. Who was this kid? What was that boat? Where the hell is New Zealand?

The 26th edition of the America's Cup regatta began with the challenger trials on October 5, 1986. The event was especially notable for the many firsts it recorded: first time the US was not the defender; first time as many as 13 teams, representing six nations, were entered; first time New Zealand had made a challenge; first time television cameras were allowed on board the racing vessels; first time a fibreglass boat was racing.

In the first round robin of the challenge trials, the teams raced each other once. New Zealand's record was 11-1 in *KZ-7*, the third boat built which incorporated improvements learned from sailing *KZ-3* and *KZ-5*. *KZ-7*'s only loss was a 49-second defeat to Dennis Conner's *Stars & Stripes*. Conner had lost in 1983 to *Australia II* with her controversial wing keel and his actions proved he had arrived in Fremantle determined to dispute any and all design elements he considered outside the rules. Throughout the trials, Conner focused on the fibreglass issue [see Chapter 5].

"Glassgate", as the journos loved to call the affair, may have generated a good deal of sound and fury on land, but it was of no consequence on the water. *KZ-7*, dubbed *Kiwi Magic* and given official clearance to continue racing, completed the next two rounds of competition undefeated and advanced to the semi-finals with a remarkable 33-1 record. She would face *French Kiss* while Conner and crew would race Tom Blackaller in the San Francisco syndicate's *USA*. The semis resulted in little drama – both *Kiwi Magic* and *Stars & Stripes* won the series with identical 4-0 scores.

Dennis Conner's *Stars & Stripes* (US-55) slams through a wave off Fremantle, Western Australia, on the way to victory in the 1987 America's Cup. Steady boat improvements, outstanding seamanship and crew work, and exceptional tactics won the Cup for the American team.

In New Zealand's only victory against *Stars & Stripes*, *Kiwi Magic* tacked over 100 times to tightly cover the American team. The fitness of the grinders was tested to the maximum. Here, *KZ-7* grinder Brian Phillimore is in action on *KZ-3*.

Going into the finals, *Kiwi Magic* had beaten *Stars & Stripes* two of the three times they raced and had now compiled a record of 37-1. *Stars & Stripes* stood at 31-7. On paper, and indeed on the water, the New Zealanders looked invincible.

But as *Stars & Stripes* jumped out to a 2-0 lead, it was apparent that the Americans had steadily improved over the four series they had sailed. Not only was their teamwork more in sync, but the major difference was that they had made substantial changes to their boat. New appendages, new spars, new sails, new sail shapes, and a speed enhancer attached to the bottom of the hull called "riblets" had all been added before the challenger finals.

The third race went to the Kiwis, after Dickson won the start and tight covered *Stars & Stripes*. Conner, ending the fairytale debut by New Zealand in America's Cup competition, won the fourth and fifth races.

On the defender side, Alan Bond's campaign to defend the trophy his team had won in Newport just three years earlier had come unglued. *Australia IV* lost to *Kookaburra III*, campaigned by the syndicate headed by Bond's arch-rival Kevin Parry and steered by Iain Murray. It was a bitter contest on and off the water.

Stars & Stripes went on to a decisive 4-0 victory over Australia's *Kookaburra III* in the Cup match, winning by an average margin of 1 minute 39 seconds. The trophy that had spent so many years in the United States was headed north once again, this time to San Diego, California.

Michael Fay, Chris Dickson and the entire Kiwi team returned to New Zealand to a heroes' reception. They shared that status with the fibreglass boats which had picked up the appellation "Plastic Fantastics". The boats and team didn't win the America's Cup, but no one would have known that, judging from the public's reaction. America's Cup fever began to spread. Almost before the parades and parties ended, Kiwis began to question how the next Cup campaign would take shape.

That was also a question being asked by potential challengers around the world. The lack of an announcement was due to a power struggle between Conner's Sail America syndicate and the San Diego Yacht Club over who would run things. While they argued, the challengers waited, slowly losing patience. One man who had long since lost patience with all things Dennis Conner and Sail America was Andrew Johns, legal counsel to the first New Zealand challenge. As the Kiwi sailing team headed for the 12-metre Worlds, he headed to the library to study historical and legal documents. In the library, Johns found what he believed was substantial evidence to conclude that the America's Cup was intended to be challenger-driven, not defender-driven. The challenger had the right to propose certain conditions of racing.

Johns advised Fay to draw up a formal legal challenge based on the guidelines of the Deed of Gift, the twice-amended, then 136-year-old document, which served as the rules of the game. Fay did just that and he and Johns headed to San Diego. The document they left with the commodore of the San Diego Yacht Club initiated the most bitter, controversial, and litigious episode in America's Cup history as a 130ft monohull was met by a 60ft catamaran. After two races the "Big Boat" challenge ended in the courtrooms.

In the space of a little more than one year, the America's Cup had gone from the zenith it achieved in Fremantle to the nadir it reached in San Diego. The Australian event sent people around the world to their television sets to watch sailors pound through what appeared to be survival conditions in the Indian Ocean. The courage of the crews, the expert seamanship exhibited, the closeness of the races, Conner's dramatic comeback, and the Fremantle festivities

Opposite page: New Zealand's "Big Boat" (*KZ-1*) campaign in 1988 was met by Dennis Conner's catamaran and both teams spent more time in court than they did on the water.

Chris Dickson in discussion with Dennis Conner during the 1986/87 challenger trials. Dickson's 37-1 record going into the challenger finals was an incredible achievement for a first-time effort.

David Barnes was skipper of the Big Boat campaign in 1988 and tactician for the New Zealand Challenge in 1992 and is now working with *America True*.

Rod Davis was helmsman for the New Zealand team during the 1992 America's Cup challenger races. He's now coaching the Italian Prada team for the 2000 Cup.

Raul Gardini and Paul Cayard are all smiles after the *Il Moro di Venezia* team from Italy won the Louis Vuitton Cup in 1992 to advance to the America's Cup match against *America³*.

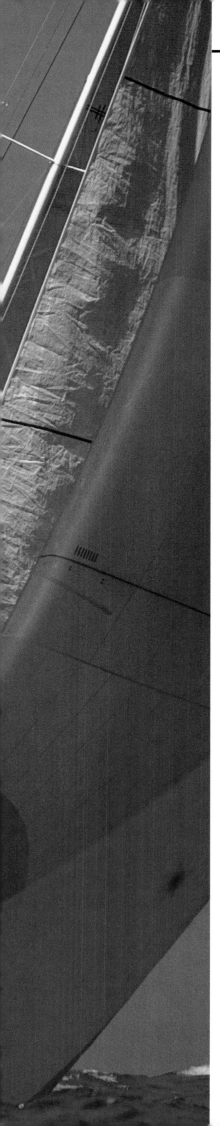

established a new fan base, only to be partially destroyed by the acrimonious mismatch.

The 1991 Worlds, and the Cup to follow, introduced many new line-ups to the game. The Kiwi star of the Fremantle battles, Chris Dickson, was steering the Japanese challenge. American Rod Davis, who had joined the New Zealanders as tactician for the victorious 1987 12-metre World Championship campaign, was now the helmsman for these Worlds. Russell Coutts, winner of the 1984 Olympic gold medal in the Finn Class, was on board as tactician. David Barnes, who had replaced Dickson at helm for the '87 12-metre Worlds, had been tapped by Fay to help manage the syndicate.

Other players in the America's Cup drama that was about to unfold were American multi-millionaire Bill Koch, whose America[3] syndicate was out to dethrone Dennis Conner as the defender. Wealthy Italian industrialist Raul Gardini headed up his country's challenging syndicate with American Paul Cayard as skipper and helmsman. Japan's Nippon Challenge was a first-time challenger, as was the team from Spain. Back in the fray were teams from France, Sweden, and Australia (with two syndicates).

New Zealand's campaign for the Cup had been long in the making and they were a favourite to win the Worlds' competition. The boat that New Zealand raced in the International America's Cup Class (IACC) Worlds was one of three built to date, with one more to follow, all under the syndicate management of Michael Fay, now Sir Michael Fay, back for his third America's Cup challenge. The team did well, but finished second to Italy.

When the challenger trials began, the Kiwis were in their newly built, fourth-edition boat which docksiders and international journalists claimed was clearly the most high-tech vessel in the entire America's Cup fleet. Two distinguishing features of the boat led these observers to their conclusion. One was the tandem keel affixed to the bottom of the boat and the other was a white bowsprit, which was fixed to the front of the boat. The principle of the twin keels was that they reduced drag and thus increased boat speed. The bowsprit made trimming and gybing reaching sails easier by reducing the amount of load compression on the spinnaker pole.

By 1992, it seemed that an America's Cup couldn't be run without a design controversy. The wing keel, the fibreglass issue, the Big Boat all caused consternation from a rules perspective. This year it was the great bowsprit debate. When the Kiwis' boat first appeared with its white spar, it immediately set off a blizzard of paper sent between race officials and the New Zealand syndicate. The issue was whether the use of the bowsprit was legal and the dissent was led by the Italians.

While the storm raged on land, the Kiwis were doing quite well on the water. Three round robins were scheduled to determine which four challengers would advance to the semi-finals of the Louis Vuitton Cup. Round one ended with both New Zealand and Nippon winning six of their seven races. New Zealand took control of first place by going undefeated in the second round, but Italy's *Il Moro di Venezia* showed her strength by losing only once and moving into second place. In the

Opposite page: The large asymmetrical spinnakers power *Il Moro di Venezia* (left) and *New Zealand* through the chop off San Diego, California, during the 1992 challenger finals. Notice the white bowsprit on *New Zealand*, the subject of a protracted controversy that eventually spelled doom for the Kiwis.

third round it was Dickson and his Japanese team who went undefeated to advance into the semis in first place while New Zealand dropped to second and Italy fell to third. France remained in fourth.

The semi-finals were notable for the collapse of the Nippon challenge. After losing just three races in the first three rounds and going undefeated in the last series, Dickson and his crew were able to manage only one win in their first seven races and were eliminated with the French after each team won just three races. New Zealand advanced to the challenger finals with seven wins to race the Italians who finished the semis with five victories.

Throughout the racing the bowsprit controversy raged, continuously fuelled by the Italians. Now that the two principals in the debate were to race each other to determine which team would sail in the America's Cup match against the defender, the dispute headed for a climax. Already there had been numerous hearings from which rule clarifications, decisions, amended decisions, and revised definitions were issued. Confusion reigned, to say the least.

In the first race of the Louis Vuitton Cup finals, Davis crossed the start line 18 seconds in front of Cayard and the Kiwis never looked back, winning by 1 minute and 32 seconds. The second race was one of the most exciting in America's Cup history. The two boats were never more than two or three boat lengths apart around the entire 20.3-mile course. New Zealand led at the first mark by 13 seconds, the second mark by five seconds, and the third mark by eight seconds. On the seventh leg Cayard outmanoeuvred Davis as the two boats converged on opposite tacks and the Italians took the lead. But the Kiwis surged back before running out of room while *Il Moro di Venezia* placed her nose ahead of *NZ-20* to win the race by just one second.

Races three, four, and five all went to the Kiwis. Now with a record of 4-1, they needed only one more victory in the best-of-nine contest to win the Louis Vuitton Cup and advance to the America's Cup match. But not so fast! It was during the fifth race, as Cayard trailed by more than two minutes and knowing the desperate situation his team was in, that he chose to raise the protest flag. The bowsprit issue raised its ugly head once more.

This time the Louis Vuitton jury ruled in favour of the Italian protest and chose to "annul" the Kiwis' fourth victory. Suddenly the New Zealand lead was cut from 4-1 to 3-1. The victory in the protest room fired up the Italians and unsettled the Kiwis. For some 35 races the New Zealanders had used the bowsprit to trim and gybe the asymmetrical spinnaker. All of a sudden they had to use whole new techniques to carry out the same sail-handling functions.

The Italians, sensing vulnerability, charged back in the next two races to tie the series at 3-3. The Kiwi camp was in disarray, illustrated by the decision to replace Davis and tactician David Barnes in the next race with Russell Coutts and Brad Butterworth. The tactic almost paid off as the new helmsman and tactician managed to win the start and take the lead at the first crossing. That advantage was maintained most of the way up the first leg until once again Cayard outmanoeuvred the Kiwis as the two boats approached each other. *Il Moro* rounded the first mark ahead and never relinquished the lead, winning by 20 seconds.

The last race also went to the Italians, giving them four straight wins since the protest victory. They advanced with an overall record of 26-12 as Sir Michael Fay and his team headed home with a 28-10 (not including the "annulled" victory) record. Three times the Kiwis had entered the America's Cup and three times they had been involved in bitter, controversial defeats.

The 1992 America's Cup match was raced between the Italians and Bill Koch's America[3] syndicate. Koch reportedly spent $US64 million of his own money in an effort that, at its core, was based on science and technology. Whether it was money or technology or organisation or preparation or just plain old sailing skills that enabled the Kansas millionaire to beat defending champion Dennis Conner is a subject for yacht club bar discussions, but there is little doubt that the two teams who contested the Cup that year were the two who had spent the most. Estimates of the Italians' war chest top $US100 million.

America³ won the match 4-1 with superior boatspeed, thus successfully defending the America's Cup and dictating that the next event would once again be in San Diego. Whether New Zealand would return was anyone's guess given the circumstances of the three defeats. The question asked by Kiwi Cup enthusiasts was, "Who would want to be a sponsor now?"

Fay, the saviour of New Zealand's original challenge and the financial force behind all three to date, had ostensibly taken himself out of the game. Stepping into the breech were Peter Blake and Alan Sefton. The two had worked together on other yachting projects, most recently the 1992 Cup campaign. Sefton had been involved in every New Zealand Cup effort and Blake had achieved an extremely high profile from his adventures in the Whitbread Round the World Race. There wasn't anyone interested in the sport of sailboat racing in New Zealand they didn't know or who didn't know them. If anyone could raise the millions necessary to fund a fourth attempt to capture the old Victorian trophy, it was Blake and Sefton.

One of the first people they contacted was Russell Coutts. The former Olympian had made a name on the international match racing circuit, rising to number-one ranking on a list that included more than 1500 sailors. He had also won the World Championship of match racing in 1992 and 1993 and had worked with Blake and Sefton on the 1992 America's Cup campaign.

Perhaps the most critical decision made in the entire campaign was hiring Tom Schnackenberg as the design co-ordinator, the man who would put together the design and sail programmes. "Schnack" had been involved in every America's Cup since 1977 when he worked with the Australians in their sail programme. John Bertrand, the first non-American skipper to win the America's Cup, credits

The 1992 America's Cup final with *Il Moro di Venezia* trailing *America³*. The picture shows the distinct difference in beam and topside flare between the two yachts.

ZEALAND

Schnack with developing the sails that powered *Australia II* to victory in 1983.

Once funding had been secured, American Doug Petersen and Kiwi Laurie Davidson were hired as the principal designers and given the responsibility to create the hull lines and the overall design concept. Petersen came out of the successful America³ effort and Davidson had been part of the design team who had created the fibreglass boats. Many other individuals made valuable contributions to the design team who included close to a dozen people.

As the design team were being formed, Coutts began to put together the men who were to sail the boat. Among the first members of the sailing team to join the effort were members of his match-racing team. They recommended other Kiwis with whom they had sailed in various regattas and before long the team began to take shape. In less than a decade, the years between the first and fourth Cup campaigns, New Zealanders had exponentially increased their profile in international competitions. The sailors joining this challenge were veterans of past America's Cups, Olympics, Whitbread races, and the international match racing circuit – all venues at which they had distinguished themselves.

For the first time in the country's history, there would be two New Zealand syndicates challenging for the America's Cup. Chris Dickson had returned from Japan and was in the process of forming a Whitbread team who would evolve into an America's Cup challenge from the Tutukaka Yacht Club. Bruce Farr, who had been a key player in the design teams of each of the previous New Zealand challenges, designed Dickson's boat. It is a testimony to Kiwi talent that Dickson's team, with far fewer dollars than the Auckland group challenging out of the Royal New Zealand Yacht Squadron, put together a very formidable effort.

Team New Zealand launched their first boat, *NZL-32,* in September 1993 and *NZL-38* followed three months later. Both boats were painted black and adorned with a large silver fern, the national symbol of New Zealand. On the boats were the words *New Zealand*, but unofficially they were called *Black Magic.* After two months of tuning and crew training in Auckland, the two boats were shipped to San Diego, ready for one more shot at winning the America's Cup.

In many respects, the 1995 America's Cup was a watershed event in the storied history of the world's most famous sailing regatta. It featured an all-women's team, a boat sinking, a three-boat defender "match", and a Dennis Conner comeback in a race for the ages. But there is little doubt that when the 1995 America's Cup is recalled in the future, the superlative performance of Team New Zealand will long be remembered. The details of the event and the New Zealand campaign are described in Chapter 3, "The 100 Guinea Cup".

Opposite page: Team New Zealand's now-famous *Black Magic* duels with Dennis Conner's *Young America* during the 1995 America's Cup match. The American defender proved to be no match for *NZL-32*, which performed flawlessly.

Co-author Russell Coutts spends his time sailing when not writing. He'll be the man behind the wheel when Team New Zealand defends its 1995 victory in Auckland in 2000.

Tom Schnackenberg and Alan Sefton are pictured here in a planning meeting, 1993. Both are back for the 2000 defence. "Schnack" (left) heads the technical and design teams and Sefton continues in his management position.

Sir Peter Blake was best known to the New Zealand public for his Whitbread Round the World successes before his involvement with the America's Cup in 1992 and 1995.

CHAPTER 2

The Perfect Venue

"We have just one wish. That the next Louis Vuitton Cup will be raced in Auckland, New Zealand."

Yves Carcel, Chief Executive of Louis Vuitton after
Black Magic won the right to challenge
for the 1995 America's Cup.

T o appreciate the true significance of staging the America's Cup in New Zealand it is first worth considering the history and the effect each different venue has had on shaping the modern regatta. During the 132 years that America successfully defended the Cup, most of the racing took place in Newport, Rhode Island. America's Cup sailing and Newport became so well connected that they were considered a permanent institution by many boating enthusiasts and indeed many of the competitors.

Whenever the event was staged people would travel to Newport not only to watch or compete in the action on the water, but also to enjoy some of the fabled parties that have become synonymous with the America's Cup social whirl. Hosting and attending lavish affairs celebrating the yachting lifestyle and promoting the uniqueness of international sport's oldest trophy became *de rigueur* among both residents and competitors. Certain invitations on land became as prized as victories at sea. After all, Newport had long established itself as the summer playground of the very rich and famous. Here was home to the mansions of the Astors and the

Above: The Model Room of the New York Yacht Club. Below: The façade of the New York Yacht Club on 44th Street in New York City. The club has an illustrious history as the defender of the America's Cup for 132 years.

Above: The San Diego Yacht Club, where Dennis Conner defended the Cup in 1995. Below: The welcoming flotilla for *America³* in San Diego.

Stars & Stripes was victorious in the typically strong winds off Fremantle.

Vanderbilts. John F. Kennedy squired Jackie about town and celebrated their marriage on the grounds of an estate overlooking America's Cup waters.

The town is proud of its link to the event. The main street is named "America's Cup Avenue". Photographs and memorabilia of past contests are still found in many of the bars and restaurants. The house where successful Australian skipper John Bertrand was said to have resided during 1983 has a simple plaque on the front door reading "John Bertrand's House". When it was Cup time, Newport was transformed. A good part of its economy revolved around the America's Cup.

But ever since Bertrand and Bond and their band of Aussies left town with the Cup, Newport has not been quite the same. While still a seafaring town in many respects and still host to many prestigious regattas, Newport without the Cup is like London without its bridge. Not quite the same. The New York Yacht Club, for more than a century conducting its business within the concrete confines of Manhattan, purchased a mansion on Newport Harbour and now has a clubhouse and dock to which members can actually bring their boats. The New York City building is still active, although the trophy room where the America's Cup was encased for so many years now seems bare without it. That empty feeling has not been lost on the membership which has generously supported efforts since 1983 to return the Cup to what it must believe is its rightful place. One wonders if the Newport acquisition is part of a grand vision.

When the event moved to Fremantle, Australia, it took on another flavour. The Australians built a special America's Cup yacht harbour to house all of the challenging and defending teams. Fremantle, previously a small, run-down fishing port, was transformed overnight into a colourful, vibrant village, spilling over with activity. The town developed an America's Cup village atmosphere where competitors, supporters, spectators and media could all share stories and mix with each other. If Newport had about it the feel of the aristocracy, Fremantle opened its doors to the common person. All were welcome and all welcomed the atmosphere.

Just eight miles from the lively city of Perth in Western Australia, Fremantle sits hard by the Indian Ocean. As a venue for the America's Cup, it benefited from prevailing strong winds, dubbed the Fremantle Doctor, which seemed to appear every day about noon, as the boats made their way to the race course. The conditions at sea consistently challenged the teams like never before and provided perhaps the best television footage in sailing history. The racing was spectacular and the event grew in popularity. The Fremantle era was short lived as Dennis Conner's Stars & Stripes syndicate put on a masterful display of boat preparation and racing skills to win back the Cup for America in 1987. The event returned to the United States, but not to Newport. When Conner and his red racer *Liberty* lost the seventh and deciding race back in 1983 to Bertrand and *Australia II*, the New York Yacht Club and its skipper parted ways. It had been a bitter summer and early fall as the many battles with the Aussies over the legality of the wing keel took their toll. Conner returned to San Diego and contemplated retiring from the Cup scene, but soon began a new campaign under the auspices of his hometown club, the San Diego Yacht Club. After Fremantle, the Cup travelled to the Southern California city where the western United States meets the Pacific Ocean, just a few miles north of Mexico.

Unlike Newport or Fremantle, small towns that offered more intimate settings, the city of San Diego did not develop a central base for the syndicates which were spread over a 10-mile radius. And in even more direct contrast to Fremantle, no doctor made afternoon house calls. The wind conditions were predominantly light, rarely blowing more than 8 to 12 knots. Such conditions would not have been favourable to the heavy 12-metre yachts used in Cup competition since 1958, so a new more powerful class was designed. The International America's Cup Class brought a new look on the water and with this and other innovative changes, the membership of the San Diego Yacht Club did their best to help the event progress, but with no central location, they were unable to create the same village atmosphere. The light

Auckland, dubbed the "City of Sails", with its spectacular Waitemata Harbour, will be host for the 2000 America's Cup.

winds also meant that the racing and the television footage was dull in comparison to Fremantle. And after the debacle of the Big Boat versus Catamaran episode that dragged the Cup through the courts, the 1992 and 1995 regattas in San Diego had lost some of their lustre. Many who started out with high hopes for the event in San Diego were glad to see the Cup finally move to Auckland in 1995.

In sailing terms, there may not be a better venue than New Zealand to bring the Cup back to its former glory. Over the past decade, New Zealand has been one of the best performing nations in many of the world's top sailing events. Through its boat building, spar and sailmaking industries, it has developed a world-wide reputation and is recognised as being one of the best countries in the world to commission a high performance yacht.

Indeed, there are high expectations that the 30th America's Cup may be regarded as the greatest sailing event ever. New Zealanders support their national sporting teams with pride and the America's Cup holds a special significance for many. The first challenge in 1987 captured the imagination of many New Zealanders and presented the very real possibility that this small country could in fact win such a prestigious prize. But no one could have predicted what would happen after Team New Zealand's victory in 1995. Approximately 400,000 people crowded the streets in Auckland alone to congratulate the country and the team. In Wellington, Christchurch and Dunedin record numbers also supported Team New Zealand in victory parades. AGB McNair's PeopleMeter system showed that 58 percent of New Zealanders aged 15 and over watched at least part of the final race on television. A further 18 percent of New Zealanders were watching in various overseas countries.

It was one of the biggest outbursts of celebration New Zealand has ever had. It seemed almost everyone, and in some cases everything including sheep, donned red socks and took to the streets in a huge outpouring of national pride.

Many described the parades as being similar to the welcome home for the troops returning from the Second World War. Team New Zealand's victory was said to be almost as remarkable as Sir Edmund Hillary's successful ascent of Mount Everest.

So when Auckland, dubbed the City of Sails, plays host to the 30th America's Cup event at the

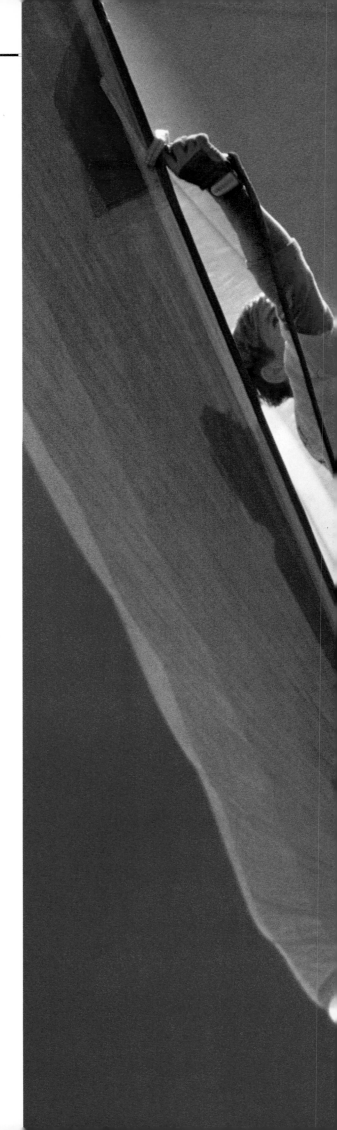

The specially built American Express New Zealand Cup Village will provide a central base for syndicate and international media.

turn of the century, it may become a party like no other. It is a city of only 1.3 million people and yet 50,000 of the people own a boat of some sort. Auckland is not new to running large regattas and has been a regular stopover port for the Whitbread Round the World Race. A Whitbread start typically attracts up to 5000 spectator boats. When the 1993 Whitbread came to Auckland, 30,000 people were at the harbour to greet the boats as they arrived, at 2 am! For the America's Cup, event organisers are expecting up to 200,000 people at the event and more than 5000 spectator craft for the America's Cup match in the year 2000.

Like Fremantle, Auckland has developed a custom-built yacht harbour called the American Express New Zealand Cup Village. This will host most of the expected 13 foreign syndicates. But unlike any Cup before, the village will be centred in the heart of the city's waterfront. It is planned that the village will also provide facilities for the estimated 90 super yachts that will visit the area during the racing. Many of the famous yachts from the past are planning visits including some of the magnificent J-Class yachts. A race to Kawau Island is planned for these and other 100ft plus yachts to take place in between challenger elimination round robins. Adjacent to the village is also the National Maritime Museum, which offers an insight into New Zealand's marine history together with information on some of the vessels, equipment and people that have contributed to the proud yachting traditions.

Those who travel to witness the America's Cup will discover that the Auckland region has a

America's Cup bases in the Viaduct Basin.
Clockwise from top: Team New Zealand, Nippon Challenge, America True, Prada, AmericaOne

Clockwise from top: The glorious Abel Tasman National Park; thrills on the Shotover River and The Remarkables Skifield, Queenstown; the Emerald Lakes in Tongariro National Park; vineyards in Marlborough and whale-watching at Kaikoura.

lot to offer. The original Maori inhabitants viewed it as a Garden of Eden because it was rich in bird and marine life. Today, while it still retains spectacular beaches and parks, the urban spread has grown to almost 80 kilometres (or 50 miles) long. This area is made up of four satellite cities: Auckland, Manukau, North Shore and Waitakere. These are situated between two natural harbours, the Waitemata Harbour and Hauraki Gulf to the east and the Manukau Harbour and fabulous surf beaches to the west. The region has over 48 dormant volcanic cones with the America's Cup course area being flanked by one of the most dominant volcanic landmarks, Rangitoto Island. In the shelter of the Hauraki Gulf, there are almost 50 islands, some of which can be accessed by ferries that depart within a short walk of the village. Auckland enjoys a warm coastal climate with average daytime temperatures during January and February of 24 degrees Celsius.

The city has a cosmopolitan feel with a large variety of top-class cuisine and entertainment. The central focus is a new international casino in the Skytower that is the tallest building in the Southern Hemisphere. This imposing structure provides a panoramic view of the various features in the area including the America's Cup harbour and course area.

Around the perimeter of the city are a number of exceptional vineyards. Some of the best are situated only a short distance from the course area on Waiheke Island. Stonyridge Larose has been rated as one of the top 20 cabernet blends in the world.

Also situated along the Waitemata Harbour are two of the countries top resort golf courses, Gulf Harbour and Formosa. In 1998, Gulf Harbour hosted the World Cup of Golf during which America's Cup challengers from Italy, America and Switzerland were seen practising on the blue waters of the Hauraki Gulf immediately adjacent to some of the most challenging holes.

But it would be a tragedy to visit Auckland and not experience the rest of New Zealand's attractions. Dunedin, Christchurch, Queenstown, Wellington, Rotorua, the Bay of Islands and the Coromandel Peninsula offer an incredible variety of activities and scenery. On the southern lakes and rivers one can fish for trout and salmon. In coastal areas such as the Bay of Islands, or the appropriately named Bay of Plenty, fishing for marlin and swordfish is possible.

The wild side of New Zealand offers many challenges to those who seek excitement. Heli-skiing, bungy jumping, white and black water rafting and para gliding are all available. For those who want to get closer to nature, several activities are alluring: swimming with the dolphins, whale-watching or hiking in one of New Zealand's beautiful national parks. New Zealanders are proud that almost 25 percent of the country remains protected as natural land and bush.

The authors recommend that the 30th America's Cup should not be missed and agree that New Zealand offers something for everyone. For the people of Auckland and indeed the whole of New Zealand, it will no doubt be hoped that visiting tourists will get more chances to view both the America's Cup racing and explore some wonderful countryside in another future defence of the Auld Mug. ⚓

CHAPTER 3

The 100 Guinea Cup

W hat is it about the America's Cup that has motivated the thousands of sailors, designers, technicians, and syndicate heads who for 148 years have aspired to win it? Personal sacrifice in the form of separation from family, friends and finances has customarily marked the quest. Fame has been elusive and other than the 134 ounces of sterling silver that constitute the 27-inch high trophy, there is no fortune awarded. Controversy, contention, and conflict have more often been the results of victory.

To understand why the oldest trophy in international sport generates such intense commitment among participants, a glance at history is necessary. While space allows only a brief outline of the 29 matches sailed under the name "America's Cup", the recounting may shed light on why this contest has become one of the premier sporting events in the world.

It has often been said that attempting to win this trophy is the biggest gamble in all of sport. Considering the vast sums of money invested in the effort, anywhere from an estimated $US15 million to as much as $US40 million a team for the 1999/2000 event, it is hard to identify another athletic contest in which so much is at stake for so little monetary return.

The lure of a big money payoff is present, but not in the traditional sense. The victorious team win the right to hold the next event at a venue of their choosing, and if managed judiciously in these days of billion dollar income projections by hosting cities, the pay-off can be substantial, but not necessarily to those who actually participated in the triumph. The losing teams return home and attempt to square things with their supporters. It's all part of the gamble.

Other than glory, personal satisfaction, potential product endorsements and a name inscribed on the trophy, the spoils of victory are ephemeral at best. Some sailors and designers will

Previous spread: A replica of the celebrated yacht *America* cuts through the sea. *America* began it all in 1851 when she won the "100 Guinea Cup" which later was named for the yacht and today is the oldest trophy in international sports.

realise a boost in reputation that can be leveraged for increased fees. Others will experience a loss of reputation.

Cup historians can make a case that the trophy and the event were born out of the urge to gamble. It is known that John Cox Stevens, a wealthy industrialist and founding member of the New York Yacht Club in the United States, was a keen yachtsman who delighted in wagering large sums of money on the swiftness of his sailboats. He was also an ardent nationalist who demonstrably supported his country at every opportunity. These two prominent character traits united in 1850 when Stevens decided to become involved in England's International Exhibition, known as "The Great Exhibition", which was scheduled to open in the following year. Organised by Queen Victoria's husband, Prince Albert, the exposition was billed as a celebration of international progress to date in the fields of science, industry and art. For Stevens, it was an opportunity to show the world some of the results of his country's industrial revolution, now yielding significant advancements since its birth at the beginning of the century.

Stevens and five friends formed a syndicate that built, in the words of the builder, "a boat... faster than any vessel in the United States brought to compete with her". Their intentions were apparently two-fold: to take the boat to England as an example of their country's boatbuilding proficiency and to take on all comers who wished to bet they could beat this newly built craft. The name of the schooner, true to Stevens' nationalistic pride, was *America*.

However, even before this "radical" schooner anchored off Cowes, word of her unusual appearance had spread along the waterfront. Considerably different from the British yachts, typically narrow and deep, *America* featured a sharp bow, wide beam, full stern, and low freeboard. Two steeply raked masts with no topsails and a single jib with no boom completed her look of an "out and outer", the term used then to define true racing craft. Despite the reaction of the 83-year-old Marquis of Anglesey, who after a close inspection uttered the now famous words, "If she is right, then all of us are wrong", that opinion was not shared by English yachtsmen.

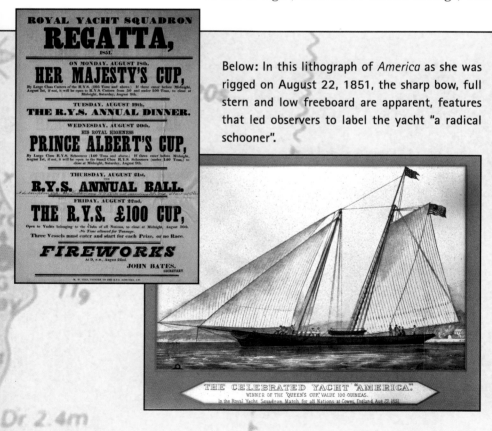

Below: In this lithograph of *America* as she was rigged on August 22, 1851, the sharp bow, full stern and low freeboard are apparent, features that led observers to label the yacht "a radical schooner".

1851

Right: John Cox Stevens was a founding member of the New York Yacht Club and the man most responsible for the creation of *America*. The original print is believed to have been made by the famous lithographers Currier & Ives.

When Stevens issued a challenge to any vessel of the Royal Yacht Squadron for a race in which he would wager the staggering amount of more than $US50,000, there were no takers.

Instead, Stevens had to settle for a fleet race "open to yachts belonging to the clubs of all nations". The race offered a cash prize worth a little more than $US500, accompanied by a rather ungainly silver trophy known as the "Royal Yacht Squadron £100 Cup" or the "100 Guinea Cup". Although called a cup, it was actually a bottomless ewer. The race drew seven schooners and eight cutters to the 53-mile course around the Isle of Wight on August 22. In front of thousands of spectators, *America* started last at 10 am, took the lead an hour and a half later, and by 5.50 pm she was 12 miles from the finish line and some seven-and-a-half miles in front of *Aurora*, the second-placed yacht. Almost three hours later after the wind had died considerably, the race was over and *America* took the honours, the cash, and the "cup".

Through the ages, the story of Queen Victoria's query about the status of the race has become synonymous with yacht racing in general, and to some extent, with the fierce competitive nature of yacht racers. Although a number of historians dispute it ever happened, the story goes that the Queen, aboard her royal yacht, asked who was winning the race. "*America*", was the reply. When she asked who was next, the answer came back, "Your Majesty, there is no second". Myth or not, there are 29 skippers of America's Cup runners-up who would no doubt attest to the truth of the statement.

While this race is the most famous in America's history, and perhaps the most famous yacht race in world history, at the time neither Stevens nor his syndicate realised the significance of their victory. Stevens was still disappointed he could not arrange a high-stakes match race, although he was somewhat placated by the growing reputation his vessel was earning, both for her swiftness and her scientific achievement. Queen Victoria and Prince Albert paid a much publicised visit to the yacht the day after the race around the Isle of Wight, a visit that went a long way towards establishing friendlier relations between the two countries and demonstrating

1857

1869

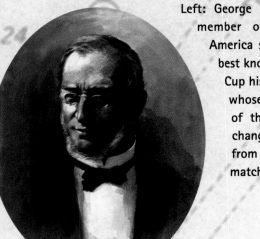

Left: George Schuyler was a member of the original America syndicate and is best known in America's Cup history as the man whose interpretation of the Deed of Gift changed the format from a fleet race to a match race.

Englishman John Ashbury's 1869 challenge was the first ever, but disputes with the New York Yacht Club over how the races were to be run postponed the actual competition until 1870. Ashbury lost, challenged and lost again the following year amid even more controversy, and eventually emigrated to New Zealand.

the potential of the developing nation on the world's stage.

America was to race only once more under the management of Stevens and his syndicate, which sold the schooner to an Englishman. When the Americans travelled home, it was with the expressed promise to return to England with another yacht, but that never happened. What did endure was the Royal Yacht Squadron's idea of "a race for the clubs of all nations".

The cup *America* won was passed among the sailors for a while, but no one was quite sure what to do with it. There were suggestions of melting it down and making medallions out of the silver for distribution to the families of the men on board. For some time the trophy was largely forgotten and was stored in an attic. In 1853, Stevens, who held the position of Commodore at the New York Yacht Club, posted "a race for all nations" with a prize of $US500. Not enough interest was shown, but the challenge was renewed in 1857. For this race, George Schuyler, a member of the original syndicate, recovered the cup and presented it to the New York Yacht Club, calling it the "America's Cup".

The trophy also came with what was intended as a simple 239-word declaration of guidelines under which future races were to be run. It is doubtful that any one of the framers of this "Deed of Gift" had any idea what conflict and discord their words would spawn over the years. The Deed declared: "Any organised yacht club of any foreign country shall always be entitled through any one or more of its members, to claim the right of sailing a match for this cup.... This notice to embrace the length, custom-house measurement, rig and name of vessel." The most famous disagreement of exactly what those words mean occurred in 1987 when New Zealander Sir Michael Fay challenged the San Diego Yacht Club, custodians of the Cup at that time, to a match in 130ft monohull yachts. What followed was bitter litigation that corrupted the hopes of the founding fathers that all subsequent races should be "a friendly competition between foreign nations".

But Fay's challenge was hardly the first to call the Deed's meaning into question. That

Above: Nathanael Herreshoff, one of the great design geniuses in maritime history, drew the lines for Cup winners from 1893 to 1920, establishing a record which may never be broken. His first boat to defend the Cup was the 124ft *Vigilant* (left) which raced with 70 men on board. Herreshoff himself was the victorious helmsman in three races against *Valkyrie II*. His last boat was *Resolute*, the first of the J–Class yachts to compete.

happened in the very first challenge proposed by Englishman James Ashbury in 1869. Initially rejected by the New York Yacht Club because it came from an individual rather than a yacht club as specified in the Deed of Gift, the challenge was renewed by Ashbury under the auspices of the Royal Thames Yacht Club.

Once officially acknowledged as the challenger, Ashbury took issue with the New Yorkers' choice of venue, their approval of the use of centreboard yachts, and their insistence that they had the right to field a fleet of yachts rather than one boat to defend the trophy. The "inside course" off Staten Island selected by the club featured strong currents, shallow waters and a good deal of commercial traffic. Ashbury, recognising that this course strongly favoured local knowledge, pushed for a race on more open water. The Englishman also argued that since no centreboarder was used in the 1851 race, "... it thereby follows that no centreboard vessel can compete against the *Cambria* in this race". Not so, said the club's negotiators who replied that that race had nothing to do with this one, citing the Deed of Gift as the new rules of the game. But then Ashbury alluded to the same document that specified that a "match" was to be held to decide the winner of the Cup. Answering his assertion that the race must be between *Cambria* and only one other, the club responded by saying that *America* had won the trophy against a fleet of vessels and *Cambria* would have to do the same.

Whether Ashbury was just too tired of arguing or whether his personal ambition got the best of him is left for historians to debate, but the record is clear that the Englishman conceded all points: on August 8, 1870, 17 boats, including centreboarders, raced *Cambria* on the inside course. The English challenger finished a distant 10th, losing to the centreboarder *Magic* after being forced to change course to avoid at least a half-dozen of the club contenders although *Cambria* had the right of way. Ashbury refused to protest, even though his yacht did suffer damage during a collision. Most historians believe a protest would have been allowed and a re-race held.

Of note is the fact that the yacht *America* sailed in the race and reclaimed some of her now-

1895

Below: It even happens to the best! As a large crowd gathered to view *Defender* on June 25, 1895, the mastless yacht got stuck on the ways. Her racing history was more successful: *Defender* beat *Valkyrie III* in three races during September 1895. Right: The Herreshoff-designed yacht *Defender*.

1914

These rare photos show Herreshoff's *Resolute* on good and bad days. Left: Sailing into the wind, *Resolute* kicks up a bow wave referred to as a "bone in her teeth". Below: The dismasting happened on July 15, 1920. The photograph wasn't found until 1946.

fading glory (it had been 19 years since her victory off Cowes) by finishing fourth.

In 1871, James Ashbury was back knocking on the door of the New York Yacht Club, but this time he came prepared. Or at least, he thought he was prepared to meet the club on its own terms. Following the disagreements over the previous year's racing conditions, the Englishman had consulted his lawyers, thus beginning a long tradition of legal involvement in what was purported to be a friendly, sporting endeavour. Ashbury's charge to his solicitors was to attack the yacht club's definition of "match" so that he could race a single boat and not an entire fleet.

Already under way in New York, as a result of both Ashbury's questioning the fairness of the match/fleet issue and unflattering comments by some American yachtsmen, the club had asked the opinion of George Schuyler, the only surviving member of the original America syndicate. Schuyler was not amused by the tactics of his fellow club members, stating: "It seems to me that the present ruling of the club [one challenger vs a fleet of defenders] renders the *America*'s trophy useless as 'a Challenge Cup', and that for all sporting purposes it might as well be laid aside as family plate."

The rebuff sent members scurrying back to the committee rooms, from which they emerged with an interesting twist on the match definition. Yes, they told Ashbury, we'll race you one-on-one, but we'll select our boat on the morning of each race. The Englishman, seeing through the obvious charade, countered that since he represented 12 different yacht clubs, there should be 12 races with the trophy going to the first yacht to win seven.

This outraged the club, which replied, "The Deed of Gift of the Cup carefully guards against any such sharp practice", a retort which served to further fuel the fire between the two parties. Ashbury responded with an ultimatum (his word) declaring that there be no reduction of the 12 races he proposed and "... the first race *Livonia* [his new yacht] won; I should in that case formally and officially claim the Cup on behalf of the club whose flag I sailed under".

The battle of words raged on as both the club and the Englishman felt besieged. Ashbury

1930

Left: Harold "Mike" Vanderbilt at the helm of *Enterprise*, which beat Sir Thomas Lipton's *Shamrock IV* in 1930. Vanderbilt was a member of one of the wealthiest families in America and was the financier and skipper of *Enterprise*, *Rainbow* (1934) and *Ranger* (1937). Below: When *Enterprise* was launched, spectators were surprised to see very few winches above decks. This innovation was enhanced aboard the 1967 defender *Intrepid*.

took offence at having his proposals termed "sharp practice" and at what he considered overall unfair treatment. Finally the two parties came to terms and the race was on.

Now the protestations of rules jimmying were transferred from land to sea. In the second race the race committee committed two stupefying blunders. First they set a course 10 miles shorter than what had been agreed upon and, secondly, they failed to include in the printed race instructions whether the yachts were to round the marks to port or starboard. They did, however, inform the owner of their defender *Columbia*, winner of race one, that he could round either way. That decision was not passed on to Ashbury, who elected to round to starboard as was traditional in England when specific instructions were not given.

Livonia was leading at the first mark and began a long, slow gybe to clear her 127 feet around the turning buoy to starboard as *Columbia* rounded quickly with a fast tack. The defender then took the advantage and sailed on to victory, prompting an immediate protest. The committee disallowed the protest, but Ashbury refused to accept the decision, declaring the series was now tied at 1-1. Matters became even more confused when the British boat won the third race fair and square and everyone now agreed the score was 2-1, but which boat had the 2 was never really settled.

Columbia was then retired and the yacht *Sappho* was brought in to easily win the next two races. Game over, declared the New York Yacht Club; we win 4-1. Not so, said Ashbury and crew; the score is 3-2. Another race was run, although the New Yorkers insisted it was unofficial and was sailed only to appease Ashbury. And although *Livonia* lost that as well, by some twisted logic Ashbury claimed the score was now 3-3 because the defenders didn't acknowledge that it was a real race. When the yacht club did not meet Ashbury on the starting line for what he said was the seventh and deciding race, the Englishman declared himself the winner of the America's Cup and demanded he be given the trophy. However, he returned home empty-handed and accused the New York Yacht Club of being unfair and unsportsmanlike.

1934/7

Ranger and *Rainbow*, winners in 1937 and 1934 respectively, exemplify the elegance of the J–Boat era. *Ranger* was the work of designers Drake Sparkman and the Stephens brothers, Rod and Olin. *Rainbow* was designed by William Starling Burgess.

He told anyone who would listen that the moral standards by which the Americans ran their races were much lower than those to which the English adhered.

Like many syndicate heads that followed, Ashbury entered the America's Cup as much to gain social and political visibility as to win the trophy. His desires were fulfilled when he secured election to Parliament. In his later life, he emigrated to New Zealand and became a sheep farmer and the first America's Cup skipper to live in that country.

Although the first two America's Cup contests did not exactly bode well for the future of the regatta, at least from the perspective of a "friendly competition between foreign nations", the next four challenges over the following 16 years righted the event. When in 1876 the Royal Canadian Yacht Club in Toronto forwarded a challenge to the New York Yacht Club, the defending club was overjoyed to accept, hoping for a new era in which it could display its understanding of fair play. Canada's 107ft *Countess of Dufferin* was simply no match for *Madeleine*, the 106ft speedster that won the two-out-of-three series by 11 and 27 minutes.

Aside from the match proving America's superiority once again, there are two points of interest in the 1876 match. One is that the boats did not start at anchor as in the previous two matches and the other is that in the entire history of the America's Cup, *Madeleine* has been the only boat named for a woman to win and defend the trophy.

Canada challenged again in 1881, but the 70ft *Atalanta* suffered the same fate as her predecessor. This time, the American *Mischief* won by 28 and 39 minutes.

The result of the two lopsided victories was a revision of the Deed of Gift after *Countess of Dufferin* and *Atalanta* owner and designer Alexander Cuthbert announced he would once again challenge for the America's Cup in 1882. The New York Yacht Club, fearing the race's death by boredom, asked George Schuyler to revisit the original Deed and correct the problems that had arisen out of the first four competitions. He added 263 words of more legalistic language that allowed the defender to enter only one boat and prevented the challenger who had lost from

1958

Left: This photo by Paul Darling is believed to be the first colour image of America's Cup action – *Columbia* crosses the finish line after beating Britain's *Sceptre*. Below: Olin Stephens, naval architect; Henry Sears, syndicate manager; and Briggs Cunningham, skipper. The three were involved in the Columbia campaign which initiated the 12-metre era.

challenging again for two years, among other stipulations. That essentially put an end to Cuthbert's hopes of racing again in a year and sent him home while New York Yacht Club members began searching for more prestigious foreign challengers.

By 1885 Britain's Royal Yacht Squadron decided to win back the trophy it had lost to *America* in 1851. But to do so, it would have to beat the team headed by two Bostonians, owner Charles J. Paine and designer Edward Burgess. The races between the 94ft *Puritan*, the first of three successful defenders designed by Burgess, and the 96ft *Genesta*, a classic narrow cutter design, went a long way towards repairing the faded profile of the event. First and foremost, the two boats were not so unequal in speed, although the final score was 2-0 in favour of the defender. But in the final race, *Genesta* took the lead twice and actually led around the last mark before her opponent caught her in 30-knot winds on the final 15-mile beat to the finish, winning by just 1 minute and 38 seconds.

The other occurrence that helped restore faith in the character of the event and the individuals who participated was the, at the time, widely acclaimed sportsmanlike gesture on the part of the British captain, Sir Richard Sutton. In the first official race (the race the day before was not concluded within the allotted time limit), *Puritan*, on the port tack, attempted to cross *Genesta* who had right-of-way on the starboard tack, and in so doing caught the British bowsprit and was immediately disqualified. The race committee advised Sutton to sail the course for an uncontested victory, but he declined, saying, "... We came to race the Cup defender and cannot accept a walk-over."

Paine and Burgess worked their magic again in 1886 and 1887, the only period in Cup history that the event was run three years in a row. In '86 *Mayflower* beat the Royal Yacht Squadron's *Galatea* by more than 12 and 29 minutes respectively in two races, and the following year *Volunteer* took out Scotland's Royal Clyde Yacht Club's entry *Thistle* by more than 19 and 11 minutes.

There had now been seven America's Cup matches raced and seven times the defender had

1962

Below: *Weatherly* (furthest away) heads to the finish line in a race with Australia's *Gretel*. The American defender won by 26 seconds, much to the delight of helmsman Bus Mosbacher and his wife Pat (right).

won easily. In fact, in the 16 official races contested, the challenger had only recorded one win (*Livonia* in the second race in 1871). Some may argue that the rules, defined and refined by the New York Yacht Club, had as much to do with those victories as brilliant designs and sharp sailing. But it is difficult to dispute that the art of building fast boats had been well learned and even better practised by the Americans.

Despite its obvious success, the New York Yacht Club was still uncomfortable with the rules and they changed the Deed of Gift once again, this time adding in 1887 what has been termed as officious, legalistic, contractual terminology. The biggest change was that the document now called for races to be held on the ocean (the venue of New York Harbour had raised the hackles of more than one challenger), over alternating triangle and windward-leeward 30-mile courses.

From 1893 to 1930, two men took centre stage and brought with them a brilliance and dignity perhaps unique in America's Cup history. Nathanael Herreshoff's dominating reign of excellence began with the design of *Vigilant*, a 124ft monster sloop that required 70 crewmen to handle her. The designer himself proved the only capable helmsman of this unique vessel and he steered her to three straight victories over the Earl of Dunraven's *Valkyrie II*. Dunraven, representing the Royal Yacht Squadron, was as argumentative as any of his challenger predecessors, and after losing again in 1895 aboard *Valkyrie III* to Herreshoff's *Defender*, he accused the New York Yacht Club of fraud when a race in which he finished first was disqualified due to a foul at the start.

What came to be known as the "Dunraven Affair" ended ingloriously in 1896 when the Earl was expelled from his honorary membership in the New York Yacht Club. With this dismissal came the end of any hopes of another English challenge in the near future, and club members began to wonder if the event was worth the rancour and disputes it seemed to engender.

Three years later, a Scotsman, by way of America and Ireland, brought light to the darkest days of the America's Cup. Thomas Lipton was born in 1850 to impoverished Irish parents

1964

Olin Stephens designed *Constellation* (left), which had no trouble defeating Britain's *Sovereign* (below, boat on right). Peter Scott, son of the famous Antarctic explorer Robert, was the skipper of England's hope to reclaim the trophy that left their country over a century earlier.

living in Glasgow, Scotland. As a boy he emigrated to the United States and eventually worked in a New York grocery store. At 19 he returned to Scotland and opened his own grocery store that became a chain and later an international success.

As Sir Thomas Lipton, he made the first of his five legendary challenges on behalf of Ireland's Royal Ulster Yacht Club in 1899. Although he lost all of them, four times to Herreshoff-designed vessels, Lipton brought an unwavering sense of sportsmanship that was previously unknown to the America's Cup competition. Naming each of his boats *Shamrock* (*I* through *V*), Lipton was an innovator who was the first to tank test a scale model before building a racing yacht (1901). Yet his inventiveness was matched by Herreshoff's brilliance and his money was overmatched by syndicates that included J. Pierpont Morgan, William Rockefeller and Cornelius Vanderbilt.

It wasn't until 1920, in his fourth challenge with his fourth *Shamrock*, that Sir Thomas managed to win his first race. Actually he won the first two against Herreshoff's sixth and final America's Cup boat, *Resolute*. Needing only one more win to capture the Cup, *Shamrock IV* did cross the finish line ahead of her opponent in the third race, but these races were conducted under a handicap system in which smaller boats with less sail area were allowed time. In that race Lipton's yacht owed *Resolute* 7 minutes and 1 second and the defender was therefore awarded the race. Lipton's heart must have broken as the Americans won the final two races easily, although he may have been somewhat consoled by the knowledge that in the 13 America's Cup matches to date, his challenge had come closest to taking the trophy home.

Resolute's victory marked the end of Nathanael Herreshoff's extraordinary 27-year America's Cup career. His contributions to the event and to the world of yacht design were vast. At 144 feet with 16,000 square feet of sail, his *Reliance* was the largest boat ever to sail in the America's Cup and some say the ugliest. His *Columbia* was the first of only three boats (*Intrepid* and *Courageous* are the others) to successfully defend twice in a row, and some say she was the

Above and right: The 1967 America's Cup match brought Australia's *Dame Pattie* (foreground) and America's *Intrepid* to the starting line. *Intrepid* is considered one of Olin Stephens' most radical (and fastest) designs, introducing a very small keel and below-deck winches.

most beautiful of all Cup boats. His "Universal Rule" revolutionised not only America's Cup racing, but to some extent, yacht racing throughout the world. His legacy is not only one of brilliance, but one of preserving and representing what the original members of the America syndicate had in mind when they created the competition: the pursuit of technical excellence.

Sir Thomas Lipton's fifth and final challenge came in 1930, 31 years after his first *Shamrock* joined the battle. Through those years Lipton had displayed an uncommon grace and elegance in losing yacht races, but he had won the hearts of an international audience. At age 80 he was still game and his fifth *Shamrock* was well designed and sailed fast, but the defender's *Enterprise* was technologically superior. William Starling Burgess, son of Edward, designed the US boat. Harold Vanderbilt was the skipper of *Enterprise*, which won 4-0. But because he defeated the man whom many credit with saving the America's Cup, Vanderbilt found no joy in victory. "Our hour of triumph, our hour of victory is all but at hand," he wrote, "but it is so tempered with sadness that it is almost hollow… " His sentiments were shared by millions around the globe.

The 1930 match was significant for two other reasons as well. It was the debut of the J-Class sloops, the graceful beauties that preceded the "modern era" of America's Cup yachts and are today a symbol of the big, powerful vessels owned by the wealthy and raced for the thrill of it. The *Enterprise/Shamrock V* match was also the first to be conducted in the waters off Newport, Rhode Island, where the New York Yacht Club would hold each of its defences for the next 53 years.

The J-Boat era was short-lived with only the 1934 and 1937 matches raced in that class. After the death of Lipton, aviation magnate T.O.M. Sopwith rose to the challenge, and his *Endeavour* came as close to winning the Cup in '34 as any boat since *Shamrock IV* and closer than any challenger to follow until *Australia II* accomplished the task in 1983. Matched against the W.S. Burgess design *Rainbow*, *Endeavour* won the first match, also the first America's Cup race to no longer use time allowances, by 2 minutes 9 seconds. *Endeavour* came back with a

1970

Left: A stern view of *Gretel II* shows helmsman Jim Hardy at the wheel of the wooden yacht Australia hoped would bring victory. She was successful in the second official race, but the reconfigured *Intrepid* won four others to keep the Cup in New York. Below: *East Chop* was one of many spectator boats that took fans close to the action.

51-second victory in race two. Race three was the turning point of the match. Sopwith had a six-minute lead at the final mark and needed only to steer a straight course to the finish line on a 15-mile reach. But Sopwith panicked, tacked to cover his opponent, and *Rainbow* blew by. After that the defender won the next three races to keep the Cup.

Sopwith was back in 1937 with *Endeavour II*, but Burgess was also back, leading a team of designers that included Olin and Rod Stephens and Drake Sparkman. The result of their collaboration was *Ranger*, the last of the J-Class boats to defend the America's Cup and one of the most dominant racers of the 20th century. In the summer of '37 the great yacht won 32 of 34 races by an average of more than a mile per race. Sopwith was sent home without a victory in four attempts, leading skipper Vanderbilt to declare that the yacht was so powerful no further competition would be found and the J-Class era would end.

The prediction was correct as events of the age, namely World War II, and a disinterest in America's Cup competition would conspire against the now 86-year-old event.

But once world peace was restored and prosperity was the goal of the 1950s, at least in America, the New York Yacht Club began to search out interest in renewing the "Holy Grail of yacht racing". The search was also on for another type of boat as even the most die-hard traditionalists came to realise that the days of the 100-footers were over.

They settled on the 12-metre, designed under Europe's system of classifying racing sailboats called the International Rule. Smaller than the boats designed under Herreshoff's Universal Rule, the 12-metre carried less sail area, eliminated centreboards, and originally was to be built only from wood. A popular boat first built in 1906, the narrow-beamed craft with a more definitive V-shape hull was adopted by the New York Yacht Club as the new America's Cup racer when it once more revised the Deed of Gift. This fourth document, validated by the Supreme Court of New York in 1956, contained two new provisions. One read: "The competing yachts or vessels, if one mast, shall not be less than forty-four feet nor more than ninety feet

1974

Below: *Courageous* with Ted Hood at the wheel and Dennis Conner (wearing white visor) calling the tactics. This was Conner's first America's Cup experience. Right: The American defender on the racecourse with *Southern Cross*, defeated in all four races.

on the load waterline." The other condition dropped the requirement that boats had to sail to the venue on their own bottoms.

If the new yacht and new rules gave potential challengers any impression that the defender might now be more vulnerable to defeat, the notion was quickly dispelled during the 1958 match between *Columbia* and the Royal Yacht Squadron's *Sceptre*. Designed by Olin Stephens and named after the Herreshoff boat that so ably beat the first two *Shamrock*s in 1899 and 1901, *Columbia* won every start but one. Of more importance, she left *Sceptre* to her stern at the finish line by an average of 8 minutes in the four official races (race two was thrown out when the time limit expired).

The 1962 match brought new blood to the America's Cup. *Sceptre*'s defeat had been so decisive that the Royal Yacht Squadron's ability to organise a competent challenge was questioned in yachting circles throughout the world. With the rule requiring yachts to sail to the competition on their own bottoms waived, sailors in the Southern Hemisphere began looking at the America's Cup seriously. When the Royal Sydney Yacht Squadron challenged, the New York Yacht Club promptly accepted, much to the dismay of the Royal Thames Yacht Club which believed it could retrieve England's reputation as ruler of the seas.

The first Down Under effort was a strong one. *Gretel*, designed by Alan Payne with the aid of American testing tanks and outfitted with US sail material and winches, won the second race and lost the fourth by just 26 seconds. Credit is given to defending helmsman Bus Mosbacher aboard *Weatherly* for employing tactics that kept the Cup bolted in the New York clubhouse, even though the Australians' boat was widely believed to be faster.

The fact that this was the first time since the 1934 match that a challenger had won a race made an impression on the New Yorkers. They quickly revisited the rules and issued a "country-of-origin" interpretation. Simply stated, this declaration demanded challengers must use facilities, products and personnel that were native to their own country.

1977

Below: It was another undefeated America's Cup match for *Courageous* in 1977 against Australia, a result that brought cheers from skipper Ted Turner (right). The flamboyant Turner is credited with attracting public attention to the event with his colourful, some say outrageous, style.

After defender *Constellation* easily beat the British *Sovereign* in 1964 (average winning margin: 12 minutes plus) and *Intrepid* went undefeated against Australia's *Dame Pattie* in 1967, the New York Yacht Club had now successfully defended the America's Cup in 20 different matches that had taken place over 97 years.

While a case can be made that the club's insistence on control of the rules governing the competition had much to do with its undefeated record, history also provides ample evidence of the superiority of American design and technology, its product pre-eminence and its dominant sailing skills. But if jiggering the rules had kept the defender a step ahead over the years, it now presented the situation in which their cunning could very possibly trip them up.

When the club selected the Royal Sydney Yacht Squadron over the Royal Thames Yacht Club in 1962, it realised that the Englishmen would be back in the near future and that they would have several years to work on design. The club therefore announced after the '62 contest that if it successfully defended in 1964, it believed, "it would be in the best interest of the sport and the competition of the America's Cup if such matches were not held more frequently than once every three years". This would give the defender, the club believed, equal time to prepare. But in proclaiming this change, the club also left open the possibility of multiple challenges, an advantage only the Americans had had since 1870. Until now, the New York Yacht Club had always selected a single challenge, mostly because only one club had forwarded its bid.

A century after the first America's Cup competition, the first multinational challenge occurred when clubs from Greece, Britain, France, and Australia challenged. Greece and Britain dropped out before the challenger trials, leaving *Gretel II*, owned by Sir Frank Packard, to fight it out with *France*, owned by Baron Marcel Bich. The Australians prevailed and were able to win one race in the Cup match against a modified *Intrepid*. The 4-1 scorecard belies the closeness of the match that many believed was a result of the challengers' trials, an opportunity to tune the boat and battle-test the sailors.

1980

Below: Baron Bich brought a Gallic sense of style to the America's Cup. Dressed in yachting white, he handles the wheel of *France 3* as Bruno Troublé scans the course. Right: *Freedom* and *Australia* were still racing at sunset in the famous 1980 "night" race.

In 1974, the New Yorkers received seven challenges, but only France and Australia built boats. The International Rule had been changed to allow materials other than wood, namely aluminium, to be used in the building of 12-metres. Australia again beat France for the right to race the defender. The 4-0 score in favour of *Courageous* over *Southern Cross* continued the American winning streak. The event was noteworthy as the debut of four of the America's Cup's most often discussed individuals: Alan Bond and Bob Miller (who later changed his name to Ben Lexcen) from Australia and Americans Ted Turner and Dennis Conner.

In 1977, the defender trials featured the sport's two most accomplished and famous sailmakers: Ted Hood and Lowell North. Hood designed and skippered *Independence* and North's boat was *Enterprise*. But it was *Courageous* who got the nod from the yacht club's selection committee and at her helm this time was Turner, the brash and outspoken Southerner who went on to build a media and sports empire and marry Academy Award-winning actress Jane Fonda. Turner's tactician was Gary Jobson who built his own career in television as ESPN's sailing commentator.

Bond was back as the challenger and although his *Australia* lost to *Courageous* 4-0, the margin of victory in each race was less than three minutes.

At age 37 in 1980, Dennis Conner had compiled one of the most impressive yacht racing records in the world. Two-time world champion in the competitive Star Class, winner of the Olympic bronze medal in the Tempest Class, the San Diego native proved his match-racing abilities as champion of the Congressional Cup regatta and as the starting helmsman and tactician aboard *Courageous* in 1974.

Conner marshalled all his talents and his considerable organisational skills in his *Freedom* campaign. In the defence trials he won 36 of 40 races against Turner, who returned with *Courageous* and Russell Long, who entered *Clipper*.

The challenger trials featured boats from Sweden, Britain, France, and Australia. Once again,

1983

Left: An exuberant Alan Bond shows his, and no doubt all of Australia's, delight as head of the first non-American team to win the Cup. Above: His *Australia II*, with the now–legendary wing keel, beat *Liberty* in the seventh and deciding race.

the finals came down to a battle between the teams led by Baron Bich and Alan Bond. And once again, Bond and Australia advanced to the America's Cup match.

The Australian boat, skippered by James "Gentleman Jim" Hardy, managed to win one race in light air, but as the wind increased to favour *Freedom*, Conner and his crew had an easy time of it.

Freedom was the last America's Cup defender designed by Olin Stephens. Even in this day and age of computer-assisted designs, design teams numbering more than a dozen people, and in some cases unlimited budgets, Stephens' record of producing fast boats remains unequalled. Beginning with his work on *Ranger* in 1937 and continuing through the 12-metre era with *Columbia* (1958), *Constellation* (1964), *Intrepid* (1967), *Courageous* (1974 and 1977), and finally *Freedom* (1980), he influenced not only America's Cup boat design but boat design in general as no other person before or since, with the possible exception of Nathanael Herreshoff. Stephens was a giant in the field and will remain a legend in America's Cup circles for as long as the regatta is run.

The 1983 match between Conner's *Liberty* and *Australia II*, designed by Ben Lexcen, bankrolled by Alan Bond and skippered by John Bertrand, was the watershed event in the now 132-year history of the America's Cup. It brought more attention to the competition than ever before and introduced the now famous "winged keel" as a design concept some consider the single most innovative advancement in modern Cup history. The Australians had to battle the British, Canadians, French, and Italians (new to the event) to win the challenger's berth. Conner's archrival Tom Blackaller teamed with Gary Jobson in the Defender campaign, which joined forces with a newly formed Courageous syndicate in an effort to depose the San Diego skipper.

By now, costs to campaign an America's Cup 12-metre had escalated astronomically. Conner had pushed the on-the-water testing and crew-training envelope to include a two-year programme. Estimated monthly costs for food, housing, salaries, sail and hull development,

1988

Left: Some called it an aircraft carrier, some called it a mistake, but Sir Michael Fay's "Big Boat" campaign was an attempt on his part to bring back the golden age of yachting by marrying the concept to modern technology. Dennis Conner's in-your-face reply was a 60ft catamaran (above).

1987

Above: The "Comeback Kid" Dennis Conner avenged his '83 loss by first taking on the largest field of challengers in Cup history and then steering *Stars & Stripes* (right foreground) to victory over defender *Kookaburra III* in four races.

among many other items, were $US200,000 a month. Masts cost between $US50,000 and $US70,000. Exotic materials like Kevlar and Mylar had made their way into sailcloth and increased costs considerably. But even so, these costs are minor when compared to the cheques the 1999/2000 campaigns are writing.

On the challenger side, *Australia II* proved to be the superboat the New York Yacht Club had long feared. Before meeting Britain's *Victory* in the challenger finals, the Australian boat amassed a 44-5 record and then advanced to the America's Cup match with a 4-1 defeat of the Brits.

But the real battle took place on land, where *Australia II*'s mysterious keel was constantly shrouded in "modesty skirts" that hid it from view. The legality and country-of-origin of the keel came into question and generated the most bitter controversy in more than a century. Finally resolved to Australia's delight and America's discontent, the affair remains one of the most discussed off-the-water issues in Cup history.

Conner's road to the Cup was not as clear-cut as the Australians'. He had commissioned two new boats to be built and had chosen the red-hulled *Liberty*, designed by Johan Valentijn, to go to war. *Courageous*, now skippered by Cup newcomer John Kolius, was 10 years old but her 6-5 performance in the preliminary defender round proved just how great a boat she was. *Defender* ended that round at 5-6 and *Liberty* was 5-5.

Between rounds all three boats returned to the shed for substantial modifications and *Liberty* began to emerge as the favourite. In the defender finals, *Defender* could do no better than a 1-9 record and was eliminated. *Liberty* then disposed of *Courageous* and the most famous match in all of America's Cup history was set: Dennis Conner at the helm of *Liberty* versus John Bertrand steering *Australia II*.

When *Liberty* won the first two races, both the keel controversy and the fears of the yacht club were somewhat abated. But gear breakage on *Australia II* had as much to do with her defeat as Conner's skills or *Liberty*'s speed. In race three, the Australian superboat gave an

1992

Il Moro di Venezia met *America³* (right) in the Cup match after eliminating New Zealand (below) in a contentious challenger final.

indication of just how super she was. Her margin of victory was 3 minutes 14 seconds, the largest margin ever posted by a challenger. Conner and crew sailed flawlessly in race four to win by just 43 seconds. Now on the verge of victory, the red boat needed just one more win.

Bertrand was over early at the start in race five. But gear failure on *Liberty* and the sheer speed of *Australia II* gave him the lead on the first leg, a lead he never relinquished. Race six was a matter of Bertrand finding wind when Conner couldn't and again the Australians turned a deficit into a lead and went on to win by 3 minutes 25 seconds.

With the score now tied, the two boats met for the deciding race on September 26. Conner opted for a timed start rather than mixing it up with his more manoeuvrable opponent. The strategy paid off with an 8-second lead across the starting line. Both boats then went in search of windshifts and *Australia II* caught the first and surged to the lead, only to watch *Liberty* regain it when the shift favoured the defender.

Conner maintained the lead and rounded the windward mark 29 seconds ahead. Bertrand's crew changed to a lighter spinnaker on the first downwind run and made up 22 seconds. Now, with just 7 seconds between the two, it was back to searching for shifts. Conner placed his boat in the right place at the right time and opened up a 57-second advantage around the third mark.

It now appeared that the defender had a substantial enough lead to carry him through the next three legs. But as the first run had shown, *Australia II* was a speedboat downwind. She began to recover some distance on the second run, forcing Conner to decide either to cover his opponent and ultimately wage a gybing duel or to gybe off to the left-hand side of the course to find the wind that had served him so well to that point.

His decision to gybe will be debated around yacht club bars for eternity and no doubt has caused Conner many a sleepless night. As Bertrand went right, the wind went with him and pushed him into a 21-second lead at the leeward mark. Despite Conner's desperate 47-tack final beat, *Australia II* stretched her lead and sailed across the finish line 41 seconds ahead of the

1995

Left: Team New Zealand's 5-0 sweep of Dennis Conner's team was the greatest margin of victory in the 144-year history of the America's Cup. *Black Magic* had the measure of *Young America* at each of the 30 turning marks in the match and gained time on 25 of the legs. Right: Designers Doug Peterson and Laurie Davidson were key players in Team New Zealand's success.

red boat. History was made. The longest winning streak in the history of world sport was over.

Conner may have been down, but he was far from out. Over the following 16 years he has dominated the event to the extent he is known as "Mr America's Cup". In those years he has won the Cup back and lost it again. At the time of writing he is preparing for an unprecedented eighth America's Cup campaign to be played out on the waters off Auckland, New Zealand. Chapter One covers in greater detail the 1987-1992 Cup competitions in which Conner played a major role. But it is the 1995 battle that brings him, and the rest of the sailboat racing world, to Auckland for the 1999/2000 races.

The 1995 event was unlike any of the America's Cup regattas that had preceded it. Most noticeable was the all-women team Bill Koch and his America³ syndicate had selected to defend

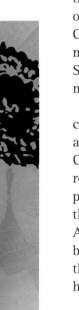

the trophy. In the 144-year history of the regatta, only three women had ever raced in the America's Cup match, serving as timekeepers. The last Cup match in which a woman participated was in 1937. Since then three other women had sailed in trial matches, but not in the America's Cup proper.

The all-women team attracted a boatload of press clippings from around the world, but so too did the anticipated re-match of John Bertrand and Dennis Conner. Bertrand had come back from yacht racing retirement to head the oneAustralia syndicate. The press liked to point out that a re-match would feature the only non-American to win the Cup and the only American to lose it. But had the Cup match ended up between the two teams, it wouldn't have been quite the same as a dozen years earlier because Bertrand had selected Rod Davis to helm the boat.

Australian Syd Fischer was back for his fourth Cup and other challengers included Japan, France and Spain and there were two challenges from both Australia and New Zealand. On the defence side, Conner was back and a group from Maine called "PACT '95" were also attempting to unseat America³, the defending champion.

With two teams entered and both doing well in the early rounds of the Louis Vuitton Cup, the Kiwi media was overflowing with news and features about Coutts and Dickson, *Black Magic* and *Tag Heuer*, and especially about Peter Blake and his red socks. Although Blake's principal role in the '95 campaign was as syndicate head and fundraiser, he did sail on the boat and when he did, he wore red socks. As *Black Magic* began to compile win after win without a defeat, Kiwis throughout the nation took to wearing the brightly coloured hosiery out of both superstition and support.

An official defeat for Team New Zealand was recorded in the second round, although it happened, not on the water, but in the jury room. Crewman Murray Jones had been hoisted up the mast throughout round one and into round two to scan the horizon for signs of wind patterns. The competitors didn't think this strategy was entirely legal and the Bertrand camp protested after their second-round race. Although the Kiwis won, the victory was disallowed on a technicality.

March 5, 1995, may live forever as the Day of Infamy in America's Cup history. When morning broke to display angry grey clouds filled with rain and wind gusts in the 20 to 25-knot range, few sailors thought they'd be racing. But the race committees for both the challengers

and defenders sent the boats to the starting line. Team New Zealand were racing *oneAustralia* that day. It was on the second beat to windward that tragedy struck and in the immortal words of John Bertrand, who responded to a press conference question, "The boat broke in half and sank. That's what happened... "

Worldwide front-page headlines told the story the next day of how *oneAustralia* had come off a series of waves when the sailors on board heard a crack. The boat appeared to break transversely behind the main primary winches. It was the worst disaster in the regatta's history, but all the sailors were rescued. To this day a number of theories are debated as to exactly why the sinking occurred. All that is really known is that the boat, representing some 20,000 hours of labour, energy and heart, still lies at the bottom of the Pacific Ocean.

Still undefeated on the water, Team New Zealand made it into the Louis Vuitton Cup semi finals and was joined by *Tag Heuer*, *oneAustralia*, and *Nippon*. Although their better boat had sunk, the Aussies displayed outstanding sailing skills by finishing the round robin series in second place.

The possibility of an all-New Zealand final in the Louis Vuitton Cup was real. Team New Zealand were a clear favourite to advance into the finals given their 22-1 record, with the only loss coming from the jury. While the oneAustralia group had 53 points to Tag Heuer's 49, the two teams were actually dead even in the win column with 17.

But the all-New Zealand final was not to be. The valiant effort Dickson and his team put together fell just one victory short. Team New Zealand won nine races to clinch first place while oneAustralia advanced to the finals with seven wins, one more than Tag Heuer.

It wasn't until the fourth race of the challenger finals, four months after the regatta began, that Team New Zealand lost their first race on the water. In the best-of-nine series, *Black Magic* had won the first three races easily by an average of 3 minutes 19 seconds. In the fourth race, *oneAustralia* crossed the start line 12 seconds in front of the black boat and maintained the lead for two hours and 23 minutes before she crossed the finish line 15 seconds ahead of the

Left: Chris Dickson at the helm of *Tag Heuer*, one of the two challengers New Zealand supported.

Below: The all-women crew sailing *Mighty Mary* came very close to winning the defender series in 1995.

Kiwis. But the Aussies were unable to force a reversal of fortune as *Black Magic* won race five by almost four minutes and advanced to the America's Cup match with a two-minutes-plus victory in the sixth and final Louis Vuitton Cup match.

On the defender's course, PACT '95's yacht, called *Young America*, finished the four round robins with 14 wins. Dennis Conner's *Stars & Stripes* posted 11 victories while the all-women team (now with a man on board) had recorded five wins. Then in the semi-finals, *Young America* continued her winning ways with nine wins in 10 races while the women's team finished the series with four victories, one more than *Stars & Stripes*.

It appeared the finals in the defence trials would be raced between *America³* and *Young America*, but in one of the most bizarre occurrences in yachting history, a deal was struck between the three defence teams to race all three boats in the two-boat final. Most observers still don't completely understand the reasoning behind this eccentric decision.

Dennis Conner once again played the role of the Comeback Kid to perfection. Not just because he escaped elimination after coming in third in the semi-finals, but mostly because of the final race in the defender trials. It all came down to a race between Conner and the women's team and when *America³* rounded the final mark and headed for the finish line some 44 lengths ahead of Conner, it seemed certain the Kiwis would be racing the women. But it's not for nothing that Dennis Conner is called "Mr America's Cup" and as *America³* sailed into a hole, *Stars & Stripes* caught a freshening breeze and overtook her stalled opponent. Conner had done it again. For the third time in the past four America's Cups, he would be racing New Zealand to determine who would raise the trophy in victory.

Conner may have pulled off a miracle, but real magic was found in the form of the black boat in the 1995 America's Cup match. It simply was no contest. The Kiwis went through May as they had in January, February, March, and April. Their 5-0 sweep of the Americans was the greatest margin of victory in the 144-year history of the Cup. The average margin of victory in those five wins was 2 minutes 52 seconds. *Black Magic* led at all 30 marks in the five races, gaining time on 25 of the legs.

The 42-1 overall record was the best ever posted by any America's Cup team. The average margin of victory in all races was 3 minutes 6 seconds. Team New Zealand gained time over the opposition in 77 percent of the 260 legs they raced and they were in the lead on 93 percent of those legs.

The victory brought the America's Cup to Auckland where Team New Zealand will defend it beginning in February 2000. The team to meet the Kiwis will come from a strong field of challengers that begin competing for the Louis Vuitton Cup in October 1999.

In his book *Course to Victory*, winning helmsman Russell Coutts wrote: "And so the fourth time was a charm. Team New Zealand built on what Michael Fay and Chris Dickson and Roy Dickson and Laurent Esquier and Rod Davis and Bruce Farr and David Barnes and a thousand others on board and ashore had done over the past 11 or so years and we accomplished the goal every Kiwi challenge had had since 1984. We did it because of what came before us, because of what collectively we'd learned on the oceans and in the design rooms and tank testing facilities and sail lofts of the world. We did it because we put the team first and we learned to trust each other totally. We did it because we all had a say in what we thought would make the boat go fast. We did it because we'd been to Admiral's Cups and One Ton Cups and dinghy world championships and the Olympics and the match racing circuit and Whitbread Round the World Races and races in Auckland Harbour. And most of all, we did it because two black boats were faster than anything any other nation could come up with.

"Pure magic? No. Team magic? Probably. A magic time? Most definitely."

It remains to be seen how well Team New Zealand will do in their own backyard. But there is little doubt observers of the five-month event are in for another magic time.

Celebration (above) turned into pandemonium (below) as members of Team New Zealand began to realise just what they had achieved. What began 11 years earlier and evolved through four campaigns resulted in finally taking hold of the Cup (below right).

Black Magic shows the winning form which brought the Cup home to Auckland where supporters will be hoping for another magic run.

CHAPTER 4

A History of Controversy

The most ironic phrase in all of sport may be the one found in the America's Cup Deed of Gift describing the hopes of the founders that the trophy would serve as a perpetual challenge cup "... for friendly competition between foreign nations". With the possible exception of the Sir Thomas Lipton/ *Shamrock* years, it hasn't quite worked out that way.

While the New York Yacht Club promised "a liberal, hearty welcome and the strictest of fair play" when it first announced it would host this new regatta, few challengers in the 132 years the America's Cup remained in New York felt either welcome or dealt with fairly. There seems to be something about the ungainly, silver ewer that breeds controversy rather than concord, rancour not respect, secrecy instead of candour. Campaigns have historically included espionage, dirty tricks, open accusations of cheating, and at times, actual litigation.

There is also an element of the bizarre and mysterious associated with the event, especially in recent years. During the 1995 campaign, a freak storm blew *Young America* off her cradle, causing considerable damage to the yacht. The French syndicate suffered a loss of $US1.5 million when the first of its two boats fell from a crane. After the costly repairs, the boat later lost her keel at sea and capsized during training. The second of the two boats was dismasted on March 5, a day that will live in America's Cup infamy.

It was on this "Black Sunday" that *oneAustralia* came off a wave in heavy winds and seas and broke in two, sinking in a matter of minutes. It was undoubtedly the worst disaster in Cup history.

The Cup has also exacted a human toll on those who have sought to win the trophy. Heartbreak and tragedy have befallen a number of individuals after their quest ended. Alan Bond's fortune played a significant role in the 1983 victory of *Australia II*, but a contributing

Black Sunday

The 1995 America's Cup will be remembered for many firsts, but perhaps none more than the sinking of a race boat. *OneAustralia* met her fate on "Black Sunday", a day on which several of the teams scheduled to race questioned the wisdom of the race committee which insisted conditions were suitable for competition.

part came under judicial scrutiny and was judged illegal. Bond followed up wresting the Cup by being arrested and sent to prison. Italy's Raul Gardini, the money man behind the 1992 Cup finalist *Il Moro di Venezia*, killed himself while being investigated as a major figure in a financial scandal. Bill Koch, who spent $64 million of his own money to win the Cup that year, was embroiled in his own scandal when six years later he was accused by the Turkish government of possessing stolen ancient coins. Koch adamantly denied the charge, but it was reported in *The New York Times* that he returned 1700 of the coins worth millions on the eve of a trial.

While such misfortunes hardly qualify the America's Cup as the Hope Diamond of sport, they do call attention to the darker side of the event. But long before the tragic occurrences noted above took some of the lustre from the "Holy Grail" of sailing, controversy and conflict had become a way of life in the America's Cup world.

It all began even before the America's Cup regatta was invented. Suspicions that the yacht *America*'s surprising victory in the 1851 100 Guinea Cup race was the result of carrying a concealed propeller led to the belief among British yachtsmen that the Americans had cheated. Although the rumour was dispelled when the schooner was hauled out of the water to repair damage to her below-waterline parts, the brief discord was a foreshadowing of disputes to come.

Six years later the New York Yacht Club sent out its announcement of a new race promising a spirit of "friendly competition... [and] the strictest of fair play". But because of the country's Civil War, the yacht club's intentions weren't put to the test until 1868 when James Ashbury of England took up the gauntlet in the hope of raising his social and political profile.

Ashbury's two challenges, as recounted in Chapter 3, were both contentious and controversial affairs. As the first two to be mounted under the banner "America's Cup", they set a precedent for many bitter arguments to follow.

After easy victories in 1876 and 1881 against two Canadian yachts designed and built by Alexander Cuthbert, the powers that be at the New York Yacht Club asked George Schuyler to review the Deed of Gift for a second time (the first was in 1871 in reply to Ashbury's insistence on defining the word "match"). The hope was to avoid problems in the future similar to those of the past four matches. Schuyler's rewrite specifically addressed Ashbury's complaints and Cuthbert's campaigns. The new Deed restricted the defender to one yacht and forever answered the numerical question of what "match" means. It also required races to be run on salt water (Cuthbert's boats were more suited to the Great Lakes), a losing boat could not challenge again for two years (Cuthbert declared after losing in 1871 he would be back the following year), and participating boats must sail to the venue on their own bottoms (Cuthbert's *Atalanta* was pulled down the Erie Canal by mules).

The new Deed survived three more events, each an undefeated victory for the defender. The third rendition of the rules of the game resulted from the 1887 match in which the Scottish yacht *Thistle* was built and launched in secrecy. After being assured the challenging yacht's waterline length would be no greater than 85 feet, the New York Yacht Club built its defender, *Volunteer*. But when *Thistle* was officially measured for the Cup races, scandal enveloped the event. The Scots were sailing a boat that featured a waterline length of 86.46 feet. Once again, the Cup was mired in a state of anger and animosity.

Although the races themselves proved no disadvantage to *Volunteer* (with two wins of 11 and 19 minutes), some members of the New York Yacht Club believed the era of "sharp practices" had returned. So once again the Deed of Gift was revised and this time the language was heavily legal. International reaction was almost unified condemnation. Even American observers viewed the new document with disdain. An American magazine covering sailboat racing called the new Deed "An Act to Prevent Yacht Racing".

The British, still feeling the wounds from the Ashbury and *Thistle* arguments, were quick to pounce. Editorials appeared, yacht club members groused, and the general public simply shook its collective head. "What will the Yanks think of next to guarantee that that piece of silver will never leave their shores?" seemed to be the general sentiment.

Previous spread: New Zealand's "Big Boat" challenge resulted in one of the most controversial mis-matches in America's Cup history.

Modern day millionaires have played as key a role in Cup history as did their predecessors. Raul Gardini (left), Alan Bond (below left) and Bill Koch (pictured below with Vincent Moeyersoms) bankrolled challenger and defender campaigns. British millionaire Peter de Savary (below right), head of the Victory syndicate in 1983. Tom Blackaller (right).

What they did think of next was to accept a challenge with the proviso that if the challenger won the Cup, it would abide by the Deed. The challenge came from a man named Windham Thomas Wyndham-Quin, fourth Earl of Dunraven, and was issued through the Royal Yacht Squadron. The Royal Yacht Squadron refused the proviso.

Lord Dunraven then began to suggest how the races should be run, with little reference to the Deed of Gift. The New York Yacht Club was astonished by the man's presumption and, yet again, angry words flew back and forth across the Atlantic Ocean.

By 1893 the conditions of the match were ironed out to the extent both sides agreed to go ahead. Dunraven's *Valkyrie II* lost all three races, but the margin of victory in the final contest was less than a minute. The Englishman proved a sore loser, complaining of unfair wind conditions and interference from spectator boats, and hinting at sabotage as a reason for his torn spinnakers.

But Dunraven wasn't finished. He returned two years later and brought the event to its knees. Dunraven claimed that in the first race against the Nathanael Herreshoff-designed *Defender*, the New York Yacht Club's boat had been loaded with illegal ballast allowing it to sit deeper in the water and extending its waterline.

An even greater controversy erupted after the second race. *Defender* and *Valkyrie III* collided at the start, resulting in damage to *Defender* which slowed the yacht. *Valkyrie III* won the race, but the race officials ruled in favour of the American vessel, citing photographic evidence. Dunraven was outraged, insisting it was *Valkyrie III* that had been fouled and after starting the third race he dropped his sails and quit, apparently in protest at what he believed was unfair treatment. After returning to England, he added fuel to the fire by openly accusing the yacht club of cheating, referring to the ballast incident.

While the New York Yacht Club was quite familiar with being accused of being unfair, an outright claim of cheating had never been proffered before. The America's Cup had hit its nadir.

Although a panel of experts cleared the club and the yacht's captain, bitterness prevailed throughout the yachting world. After expelling Lord Dunraven from honorary membership, the New York Yacht Club began seeking foreign challengers, but none was forthcoming. For four years, America's Cup waters seemed poisoned and many observers began to think the event would never happen again.

It was Sir Thomas Lipton who saved the Cup from ignominy. His five *Shamrock* challenges, from 1899 to 1930, helped restore an aura of sportsmanship and his grace and general goodwill elevated the competition to what must have been the original intent of the event's founders.

The five matches in which Lipton was involved are noteworthy for reasons other than the Cup's return to glory. The defender in each of the first four regattas was designed by Nathanael Herreshoff whose genius was responsible for a record six victories in America's Cup competition. The fifth ushered in the elegant era of the majestic J-Class yachts. The period in which Lipton bankrolled his *Shamrock*s also saw American participation by representatives of families who controlled enormous wealth: Vanderbilt, Rockefeller, Pierpont Morgan.

But true to what was becoming a Cup tradition, the period was not without its controversies. One of the most infamous was generated by a Bostonian named Thomas Lawson. A stock market speculator who had made and lost and made again several fortunes, Lawson underwrote the design and building of a yacht called *Independence* that he had every intention of entering in the 1902 America's Cup. Although repeatedly informed by the New York Yacht Club's race committee chairman that since he was not a member of the club the only way his boat could be entered was if he leased it to a bona fide member, Lawson paid no attention to the suggestion. Instead, he took his case to journalists, declaring the America's Cup belonged to the nation, not to the yacht club and any American should have the right to race. There was much more smoke than fire to the entire affair, especially considering that *Independence* was a dog of a boat that was dismantled even before the Cup races began, but Lawson's nationalistic stand did receive a good deal of play in the press.

If the brief J-Class era (1930-1937) was the "Golden Age of Yachting" as many historians have observed, it also is remembered for a match that threatened a return to the unpleasantness of the Dunraven controversy. In the fourth race of the 1934 contest between *Rainbow* and *Endeavour*, two incidents occurred that brought into question possible favouritism on part of the New York Yacht Club's race committee.

During the pre-start, Harold Vanderbilt aboard the defender and Thomas Sopwith steering *Endeavour* barely avoided colliding with each other. Each skipper believed the other was at fault, but no protest flag was raised. Then, as the boats rounded the first mark with *Endeavour* in the lead, *Rainbow* began to overtake her. Sopwith luffed his yacht to prevent Vanderbilt from sailing through, believing the rules allowed this manoeuvre. *Rainbow*, however, did not head up as Sopwith expected but instead held her course. Fearing a collision, the Englishman quickly bore off, giving Vanderbilt a clear lane to take the lead and eventually the race.

Defender, which was involved in several controversial incidents, including colliding with *Valkyre III* which led to bitter accusations by Lord Dunraven.

When *Endeavour* crossed the finish line, her crew raised a protest flag. Both Sopwith and Vanderbilt believed the rules permitted their actions, but both agreed the dispute really came down to a judgement call. However, the protest was never heard because the race committee cited a rule that said a protest flag must be flown "promptly" after the protested incident. Sopwith was sure he would have won the protest and the race, giving the challenger a 3-1 score, just one win short of returning the America's Cup to England. The race committee's decision to stand on a technicality at such a critical moment in Cup history enraged Sopwith and even dismayed Vanderbilt. The press agreed, writing scathing editorials of what seemed to be the win-at-all-costs mentality that had taken hold of the race committee members. A headline of the time gave voice to this opinion: "Britannia Rules the Waves, but America Waives the Rules."

It wasn't until several months later that the facts about the committee's decision were made public. The incident during the pre-start occurred right in front of the committee boat and was judged clearly to be Sopwith's fault, a judgement confirmed by photographic evidence. Had the committee heard the protest, they would have disqualified *Endeavour* for that incident, making the second one inconsequential. By citing the technicality, the committee were trying to avoid a possible contentious situation. Instead, they caused one. While their intentions may have been good, their tactics were not.

Following the final J-Class race in 1934 between defender *Ranger* and *Endeavour II*, the America's Cup went into a hiatus for two decades. World War II was the major factor in the discontinuance, but the cost of these regal yachts and the dominance of the Americans discouraged even the wealthiest and most competitive would-be challenger.

By 1956, the Deed of Gift was once more amended, this time in an effort to "downsize" to boats about 65 feet in length. The J-Class boats had broken the bank, so to speak, and there was a realisation that the post-war world economy could not really accommodate behemoths like this class or their predecessors. Thus began the 12-metre era which lasted until 1992, a good run in terms of longevity, if not grandeur.

While practicality changed the face of the America's Cup for the second half of the 20th century, it also bid adieu to the days when extremely wealthy individuals controlled every aspect of a campaign. With the possible exception of Bill Koch's chequebook domination of the 1992 America³ syndicate, the modern America's Cup has become a contest for corporations, and in some cases, governments. As campaign budgets skyrocketed to support sophisticated research and design programmes and the reliance on technology and space-age materials, marketing acumen became as essential as sailing skills. To accommodate the corporate approach to fundraising, Cup rules were tweaked a bit to allow first for tax write-offs and later for all-out commercialisation. Purists decry the advertising tie-ins and the logo-filled sails and hulls, but pragmatists recognise the necessity of corporate support.

The move to 12-metres kept the Cup alive and the matches in 1958, '62, '64, and '67 were relatively controversy free, although not totally without a few squabbles. Yet outside of the Lipton years, those matches are best remembered for what happened on the water, not on land. While the defenders continued the longest winning streak in international sports competition, the emphasis was on promoting fair play and cultivating good fellowship within the sailing fraternity.

That all changed in 1970 when the Australians returned to Newport, Rhode Island, for their third attempt at relieving the Americans of the ornate trophy. Led by the Aussie publishing mogul Sir Frank Packer, unsuccessful in his *Gretel* ('62) and *Dame Pattie* ('67) campaigns, the men from Down Under had sailed well and partied better. Their hearty "glad ta meet ya, mate", rough-and-ready style contrasted markedly with the more refined, some might say stuffy presence of the New Yorkers.

The challenger position did not automatically go to *Gretel II*. For the first time challenger trials were held when Frenchman Baron Marcel Bich threw his Gallic hat into the ring. A former door-to-door salesman who had made millions selling his Bic ballpoint pens to the world, Bich brought a European flair to the game. Although there wasn't much to be said about his success on the water, many have remarked about his style. He spent lavishly, enjoyed the good life and plenty of French wine and in the final trial race he took the helm dressed head to toe, gloves included, in yachting white.

Gretel II had little trouble emerging as the challenger and almost immediately her syndicate members began to complain about the Americans' approach to the Cup match. Two issues were raised before the racing began. In an effort to reduce weight, the crew of the defender *Intrepid* had removed the door to the yacht's toilet, an act the Aussies considered a violation of the cruising component of the International Rule. They were more adamant about the fact that the rudder had been hung beyond the measured waterline, attached to the keel by plastic fairing strips. Although this increased the waterline and rendered the boat, in the estimation of the challengers, a "12 and ¹/₄ metre", the New York Yacht Club measurers didn't see it that way. Clearly irritated, the Australians continued to press their case until both the fairing strips and toilet were altered somewhat.

Then came the real dispute. In the pre-start of the first race, *Gretel II* clearly fouled *Intrepid* twice. Both boats raised protest flags, but the race committee, ever mindful of the club's historical reputation in Cup protests, disallowed them both in an effort to be fair. The Australians had a few words about the decision anyway, but most observers believed they could have easily been disqualified and wondered if they really knew the rules.

That question was asked again after the second race in which the challenger collided into the defender's port side, causing damage. *Intrepid* gained the lead, but was later overtaken by *Gretel II*, which eventually won the race. Then the fur began to fly. The next morning a contentious protest meeting was held and the committee, made up entirely of members of the New York Yacht Club, ruled that the challenger was at fault and awarded the race to *Intrepid*.

The Australians were outraged and the press took up their cause: "*Gretel* Robbed" was a popular headline Down Under. When American editorialists who had little understanding of the arcane rules of yacht racing joined in sympathy and even the American ambassador to Australia publicly questioned the ruling, observers began to wonder if a sailboat race could generate an international incident.

Although war didn't break out, the Australians continued to hold a grudge, even though knowledgeable sailors concurred with the committee's judgement. Later reports indicated that when the race was over, the *Gretel II* navigator pulled out a rule book and read the relevant section to his mates. The crew realised immediately the fault was theirs but still the Aussies and their backers pointed the finger at a race committee on which no one but New York Yacht Club members sat. And even when the club resolved to change the makeup of future America's Cup race committees to an international jury without representatives from the challenging and

Secrecy took on a new image in 1983 as *Australia II* arrived in Newport, Rhode Island, with a wing keel that was hidden behind "modesty skirts" until the night the yacht won the Cup. Maestro Alan Bond conducted the skirt raising ceremony which left the keel exposed to the world.

defending nations, the Aussies remained angry and vowed to seek revenge.

Their revenge came in 1983 in the form of a wing keel. Although this design characteristic proved to be a genuine breakthrough, it was also the subject of the most bitter controversy in the Cup's 132-year history. All the protests, arguments, scandals, disputes and acrimony of the past were but a mild prelude to the land battle that erupted during the 25th edition of the America's Cup.

When the Australians arrived in Newport for their seventh challenge, they brought a "modesty skirt" that hid the keel and rudder of *Australia II* from view. It didn't take long before everyone knew something was up, or better said, down. But just what that was was a very closely guarded secret. Rumour spread along the world's docks even before the Cup season began that designer Ben Lexcen had achieved the breakthrough all designers work towards and when the challenger trials began and *Australia II* won 11 of her first 12 races, the rumours seemed confirmed.

Over on the defender's side, the New York Yacht Club selected *Liberty* and her skipper Dennis Conner in the hope of keeping the longest winning streak in international sport alive. And even before *Australia II* had won the right to challenge, the New Yorkers were determined to find out exactly what was beneath her modesty skirt.

The first visual evidence that *Australia II* was different from every other 12-metre ever built came in a phone call in mid-June to *Liberty*'s designer, Johan Valentijn. The call was made from a boatyard where the Australian yacht had been hauled out to be measured and a yard worker explained to Valentijn that he had seen the secret keel and it had wings made of lead. When the designer relayed the news to Conner, the skipper met with the chairman of the America's Cup committee at the New York Yacht Club. Conner explained he believed the secret keel did not conform to the 12-metre Rule and that *Australia II* was thus illegal. The chairman asked for more information and at first didn't seem overly concerned. But by the time *Australia II* had posted a record of 21-3 in the first two rounds of the challenger trials, the defenders began to suffer from anxiety attacks.

What followed was a series of generally misguided actions on the part of the New Yorkers who were outmanoeuvred time and time again by the crafty Aussies. As rumour, solid information and research combined to give the yacht club members a pretty good picture of what they were up against, the initial strategy was to fight the keel on two fronts. One was to go to the international measurers and argue that the keel did not meet the provision in the 12-metre Rule that a yacht "shall not draw more than nine feet". The defenders argued that when *Australia II* heeled in a breeze, she drew more than nine feet. The measurers dismissed the argument out of hand, saying they had measured the yacht according to the Rule and it met all provisions. Besides, they pointed out, yachts were measured vertically, not when they were heeling.

The second ploy by the defenders was an attempt to confirm the story that the keel had actually been designed in Holland, a clear violation of the domestic design clause in the Deed of Gift. A telegram was sent to the Dutch, reading in part: "Understand you... are responsible for development and design of special keel for *Australia II*. We... would like to build same design under one of our boats... "

The Dutch, of course, immediately informed Australian syndicate head Alan Bond of the communiqué and that was all the Aussies needed to counter-attack. They made the telegram public and declared they had caught the Americans red-handed trying to "purchase a non-American, Australian keel design... " The Americans insisted that they were merely trying to get the Dutch to acknowledge they were involved in the design. But no matter what the intent was, the scheme backfired. As Conner later said: "Here we were, trying to prove the keel was illegal, but asking them to build us the same thing. It made the club look like a cheat and a fool simultaneously."

As *Australia II* continued to win on the challengers' course, the Americans continued to

press the illegality issue, which also served to bring them further condemnation. Here they go again, the sailing world seemed to say. The New York Yacht Club is changing the rules to assure a victory. From a public relations perspective, the yacht club couldn't and didn't do anything right. But from a purely technical perspective, there did seem to be enough evidence emerging to prove that a Dutch engineer had suggested the wing keel and that Dutch facilities had been used to help design and test the keel.

The controversy took on a life of its own. The Aussies grew more and more indignant that they had passed all measurement tests and that the club couldn't stand the thought of losing to a smarter team with a faster boat so they were declaring rules violations as a last resort. The public seemed to agree and the whole situation became increasingly ugly.

In a last-ditch effort to prove its case, the club gave Bond an affidavit in which he was to swear he hadn't violated the rules. Bond refused to sign it, which led the club's America's Cup Committee to vote on whether or not to race. Although the result was to go ahead, the fact that a vote was taken at all led to claims of poor sportsmanship from many quarters.

The races were run and in what was the closest and most exciting action ever in the regatta, the Australians made good their vow to return home with the trophy. Considering the long history of unpleasantness, accusations, litigation, scandal, and just plain ill will, there was no doubt relief among the tears inside the New York Yacht Club the day the America's Cup went Down Under.

But the new address of the Cup didn't do much to end controversies. Time has made it clear that disputes concerning rules and race committees and syndicate actions were not restricted to the New York Yacht Club. The Fremantle America's Cup in 1986/87 featured the infamous Dennis Conner quote about the New Zealanders' fibreglass boats being built in order to cheat. Asked at a press conference what he thought about the plastic boat, Conner blurted out: "The last 78 12-metres built around the world have been built in aluminium so why would you build one in fibreglass unless you wanted to cheat?"

This opinion was immediately met with a firestorm of criticism from New Zealanders aimed at Conner. Sports fan or not, no self-respecting Kiwi was going to take an insult like that lying down. Newspaper editors, television journalists and the public at large denounced the American skipper. For his part, Conner said he regretted his statement as soon as he said it. In his book *Comeback*, he wrote of the incident: "I've eaten my share of leather over the years for things I've said, but there are still times I can't keep my foot out of my mouth."

But without doubt the mother of all controversies occurred when New Zealander Sir Michael Fay issued his "Big Boat" challenge to the San Diego Yacht Club. The challenge generated several years of the most heated and acrimonious arguments ever heard, arguments that still rage as a result of two American courts presenting conflicting verdicts as to who rightfully won the Cup.

The Deed of Gift clearly encourages challengers to initiate a competition as long as they meet certain criteria. Among that criteria is that the waterline length of the boat in which they are challenging be not less than 44 feet or more than 90 feet. Based on the principle that the challenger has the right to propose certain conditions of racing, Fay envisioned a glorious battle of behemoths, monohulls more than 130 feet in length overall, that would recall the golden age of yachting while built with the advanced technologies and materials of the modern day. His vision wasn't shared by the San Diego Yacht Club.

It took only 12 days after the challenge was issued before the Royal Perth (Australia) and Royal Burnham (England) yacht clubs announced they would join the "Big Boat" challenge as well. However, the San Diego Yacht Club at first refused to respond to the challenge and then, when pushed by New Zealand, rejected it. Fay's response was to petition the Supreme Court of New York, the legal custodian of the Deed of Gift, requesting the challenge be recognised.

On November 25, 1987, Judge Carmen Beauchamp Ciparick ruled that the challenge was legal and she disallowed the San Diego Yacht Club's request to make 12-metre yachts standard. The yacht club responded with pronouncements of their own, first stating that no other challengers would be accepted, then saying they would (too late to build boats), and saying the races would be in Long Beach and then saying no, they'd be held in San Diego.

The shocker came when Dennis Conner announced he would meet the New Zealand "Big Boat" challenge in a 60ft catamaran. New Zealand went back to court requesting that San Diego be ordered to defend the Cup in a 90ft waterline boat. This time Judge Ciparick ruled that New Zealand's suit was premature. In essence she said, go race and if you have protests, come back and see me.

So they raced, a giant monohull dragging tons of keel through the ocean against a multi-hull craft that skimmed over the water's surface. It was, in Fay's words, a "mismatch" that was played out to a foregone conclusion. The catamaran won by more than 18 and 20 minutes respectively in the two races. With the racing over, it was back to court to see the judge. The general opinion of the yachting world agreed with the Royal Perth Yacht Club and the New York Yacht Club, the two previous trustees of the America's Cup. In opinions submitted to the court, the clubs wrote that they believed the San Diego club was in breach of its obligations as a trustee of the Cup and that the races did not constitute a "match" as the term was used in the Deed of Gift.

The lawsuit dragged on for what, to the sport's followers, seemed forever until Judge Ciparick ruled in favour of New Zealand. For one brief moment in America's Cup history, the trophy belonged to the Kiwis. But that ruling was soon overturned by the New York Court of Appeals, forcing New Zealand to return once again to San Diego in 1992 if the Kiwis wanted to try to win the Cup.

While all the squabbling and litigation was going on, one positive advancement was made. In order to ensure that totally different designs would not race each other again, America's Cup officials reached agreement on a number of issues pertaining to future regattas. Chief among

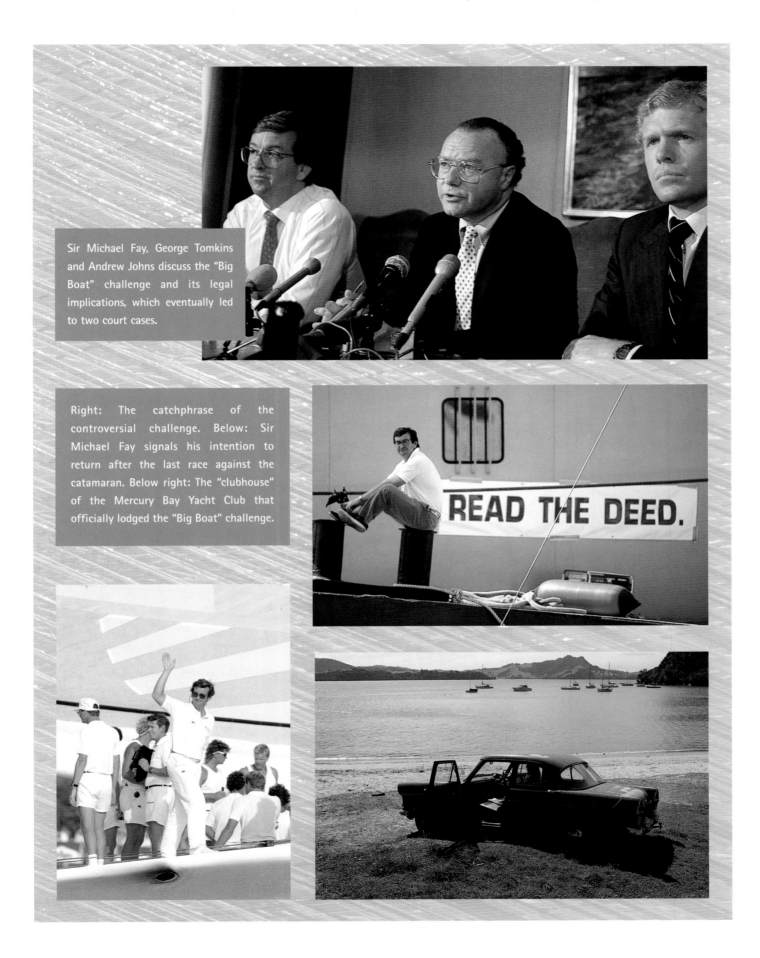

Sir Michael Fay, George Tomkins and Andrew Johns discuss the "Big Boat" challenge and its legal implications, which eventually led to two court cases.

Right: The catchphrase of the controversial challenge. Below: Sir Michael Fay signals his intention to return after the last race against the catamaran. Below right: The "clubhouse" of the Mercury Bay Yacht Club that officially lodged the "Big Boat" challenge.

READ THE DEED.

New Zealand's "Big Boat"
LENGTH ON DECK: 116 ft
BEAM OVER WINGS: 26 ft
DISPLACEMENT: 38 tonnes
LENGTH WATERLINE: 90 ft
DRAUGHT: 21 ft
KEEL WEIGHT: 26 tonnes
MAST HEIGHT: 153.5 ft
LENGTH OVER RIG: 132.8 ft

Inset: The 60ft catamaran.

these issues was the formation of the International America's Cup Class with design parameters for the new boat to be used in the races.

Although 12-metre yachts had been the face of the modern America's Cup for almost 30 years, by 1988 they were criticised for being too heavy and short on sail area. By contrast, the IACC boats at 75 feet, with 70 percent more sail area and 30 percent less weight, were promoted as speed machines.

The IACC boats made their debut in San Diego in May 1991 at the World Championships. Nine yachts, two of which were the products of New Zealander Bruce Farr, represented the new design. Farr had gained an international reputation as one of the world's elite designers whose boats had won races in all parts of the globe in dozens of classes. He had designed the "Big Boat" raced in 1988.

The 1992 Cup is remembered for Italy's questioning of the bowsprit on the New Zealand boat, a lengthy and bitter protest that many believe threw the Kiwis off their winning stride and ended with the Italians challenging for the Cup.

The 1992 races are also remembered for the "Great *Guzzini* Caper." In the midst of continued complaints about "spying" from the challengers, Bill Koch's defending syndicate, America³, following denial after denial, decided to play off the opponents' fears. At the centre of the spying accusations was a notorious 30ft powerboat Koch's team had named *Guzzini* after an Italian clairvoyant who, they claimed, could look into the eyes of the enemy and know his intentions. The allusion was for the benefit of Paul Cayard, skipper of the Italian Il Moro di Venezia syndicate, who was leading the spy allegation charge.

As the claims of spying escalated, the media became interested and began running "espionage" stories, most of which focused on *Guzzini*, which America³ personnel freely admitted was used for photographic reconnaissance, albeit from a legal distance.

Below: Kiwi bowmen work to hoist the gennaker that was attached to the bowsprit. It was this manoeuvre that caused opponents, especially the Italian team, to cry foul.

America[3] beat the Italian challenger 4–1 after Cayard and the Italians had alleged that the defenders were using high–tech spying equipment.

Photographing the opposition's boats had become almost an accepted tradition long before 1992 and had been undertaken by everyone from scuba divers to helicopter hangers with long lenses.

Once the media became involved, America³ fitted out *Guzzini* with an array of high-tech antennas, including a flat-black construction on the foredeck made of metal pie-plates and swirls of wire. Looking for all the world like a high-tech craft direct from the secret agent dock, the boat was the talk of San Diego for some time. How many observers will admit to understanding that bakers could make more sense out of *Guzzini*'s new wardrobe than could the James Bonds among the spectators will never be known, but the humour certainly wasn't lost on the *America³* crew. In fact, they took it one step further several days later, this time at the expense of a fellow defender.

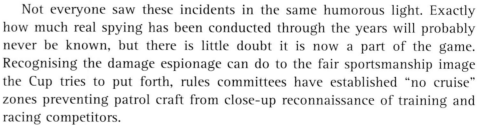

Above: Bill Koch, fresh from a ceremonial dunking in the waters where his *America³* won in 1992, rejoices with the prize most sailors covet.

Below: Cameras on *Guzzini* – a hoax or spying?

As *Guzzini* patrolled the waters one day, a deckhand spotted through long-range binoculars Bill Trenkle, Dennis Conner's operations chief, playing computer poker. He zoomed in on the layout of the cards, then called up Conner's tender on the radio to advise Trenkle: "Keep the King, discard the Jack."

Within hours, the diversion had escalated into a major international incident. Word spread to the managements of all syndicates that Koch had somehow tapped into the electronic systems of all his competitors. Phone calls were exchanged, calling for an espionage oversight committee to be formed immediately. Koch's reply was that Trenkle lost the game anyway. So much for our advice, he muttered during spasms of laughter.

Not everyone saw these incidents in the same humorous light. Exactly how much real spying has been conducted through the years will probably never be known, but there is little doubt it is now a part of the game. Recognising the damage espionage can do to the fair sportsmanship image the Cup tries to put forth, rules committees have established "no cruise" zones preventing patrol craft from close-up reconnaissance of training and racing competitors.

How well these regulations work were tested in Auckland harbour in 1998 when Team New Zealand took exception to the distance at which craft from the Japanese syndicate followed their black boats. Heated words were exchanged on the water and when the offending craft did not give way, the Kiwis rammed it. The incident made some noise in the press, but once tempers cooled and territory was established, it was laid to rest. However, it did serve as a constant reminder that the espionage issue remains as controversial as ever.

Even before the 1995 Cup began, rumblings over the newly instituted two-boat rule were heard among challengers and defenders alike. After costs got out of hand in 1992, the two-boat rule was an attempt at levelling the playing field for all competitors. But when oneAustralia and Syd Fischer's syndicate announced in 1994 they would share certain design help from a company called Fluid Thinking, cries of "foul" quickly spread. A number of the challengers and defenders objected to this, saying that this circumvented the rule that prevented each syndicate from building more than two new boats. It was argued that Fluid Thinking was designing one boat for Syd Fischer and a further two boats for John Bertrand. Fischer's boat would be tested against Bertrand's first boat before a second boat from Fluid Thinking was designed. Therefore, it was said that Bertrand in particular would effectively have the benefit of a three-boat campaign. Fischer and Bertrand vehemently denied the accusations.

As the battle of words raged on, the international jury became involved well after the third boat had begun construction. The jury sided with the Australians to the discontent of almost every other challenger and the defenders, but soon a new controversy arose. After the Nippon Challenge's first new boat of two was severely thrashed in the IACC World Championships, it became evident major reconstruction was going on behind closed doors in their compound.

Then Team New Zealand received what they determined was a reliable report that two halves of an IACC boat were being built in Los Angeles. Not long after the report, the Kiwis watched as two large portions of what appeared to be an IACC yacht were delivered to the Nippon compound under the cover of darkness. The Kiwis discussed the spirit and intent of the two-boat rule among themselves and reached the decision to lodge an official protest. The question came down to just how much refinement can be done before an "old" boat becomes a "new" boat. They reasoned that while changing a keel or a rudder seemed within the rules, wasn't changing the bow, the hull and the stern really making a new boat?

When the protest was made public, Peter Blake called the boat the "*Nippon* Clip-On". That infuriated Nippon's Peter Gilmour, who said the Japanese team had been deeply offended. As tempers flared, the international jury met again and ruled that competitors could change their boats as much as they wanted. The Kiwis didn't agree.

But as far as controversies go, the decision by the three defenders to allow three boats in the traditional two-boat final was the event that rocked the sailing world. To the challengers, press, aficionados and sailors throughout the world, "the deal", as it has come to be known, is difficult to understand. Imagine what the casual observer must have thought!

As we look to Auckland for America's Cup 2000, already squabbles among the challengers have broken out. Compared to America's Cups past, these squabbles are hardly incendiary and have had little impact on the lead-up to the overall event. With the possible exception of a brief flare-up over television broadcasting, it appears that should any real controversies arise that might have a bearing on the outcome of either the Louis Vuitton Cup or the America's Cup, they will occur during the racing itself. And that, given the event's history, is a distinct possibility! ‡

The yacht Marc Pajot and his crew have been training on was originally designed for the 1995 America's Cup and may be chartered by the Le Defi Sud team from France. The controversial question will be whether the boat has received extensive remodelling in Switzerland. If so, this might be a violation of the "country of origin" rule. FAST 2000 insists this was not so.

CHAPTER 5

For the Defence

~

Team New Zealand

Team New Zealand's victory in the 1995 America's Cup has been described as the most dominating performance in the 148-year history of the event. The 37-1 record on the water (one victory changed to a loss in the protest room) in the Louis Vuitton Cup demonstrated the superiority of the team. In winning the Cup 5-0, *Black Magic* led at all 30 marks and gained time on 25 of the 30 legs. Historically, teams have been able to develop a performance improvement between Cups of approximately 2 to 3 minutes. In Team New Zealand's case, *Black Magic* would have most likely beaten the previous America's Cup winner by over 6 minutes.

Most competitors and observers agree that Team New Zealand did indeed bring the game to a new level. After the vast amounts of money spent by the Italians, Americans and Japanese in 1992 (an estimated combined sum of over $US200 million), Team New Zealand's budget (approximately $US14 million) was small in comparison and yet the advantage gained was the most significant. The result was even more impressive considering that New Zealand is a country of only 3.5 million people and seemingly did not have the same levels of technology available.

After the Kiwis' loss in 1992, many doubted that corporate New Zealand would support another challenge. Michael Fay, although no longer wishing to invest his own money, was keen to see the

New Zealanders put to use what was learned in the previous nine years of campaigning. Scott Chapman and Ross Blackman, who worked for Fay before 1992, were retained to help Peter Blake and Alan Sefton raise corporate support in the early sponsorship stages. Blake and Sefton were encouraged enough by the response from potential sponsors to formally mount a challenge. Blackman stayed on and worked as business manager for Team New Zealand.

The Blake/Sefton combination was highly regarded in New Zealand. They had worked together in many of Blake's campaigns, including the successful *Steinlager 2* campaign in the Whitbread Round the World Race, during which Sefton worked as a personal assistant to Blake. Sefton, a highly respected journalist originally from Wales, had developed a good knowledge of the New Zealand yachting history and psyche. It was considered that Blake had the image, reputation and key relationships with companies such as Lion Nathan to gain initial corporate support. Understanding that television exposure was key to inducing corporations, the team of Sefton, Chapman and Blackman developed the initial sponsorship structure that included Television New Zealand as the central focus. Television New Zealand, Toyota, Steinlager and Enza, all sponsors of Fay's 1992 campaign, were persuaded to stay on as primary sponsors for 1995. Lotto became the fifth company to complete the "family of five" sponsors.

As the financial side of the fledgling campaign began to develop, Russell Coutts was hired as skipper and the sailing side of the challenge began to gain momentum. The first project Coutts started was a study of the factors that had contributed to earlier Cup victories. Many of the successful and unsuccessful teams were interviewed by Coutts and Tom Schnackenberg. The two documented the lessons learned and it was realised at an early stage that, with new budget constraints, there would be little or no room for wrong decisions. Former skippers, designers, technicians, builders, and syndicate heads spoke freely and revealed that many of the America's Cup teams (including some of the previous winners) had wasted more than one third of their budgets chasing projects that were fundamentally flawed or too time consuming.

Many of the key personnel choices were made during this interview process and the shape of the team began to form. New Zealand had gained much experience from its previous campaigns but it was generally acknowledged that fresh talent would also be beneficial. One of the first major departures from the previous New Zealand efforts was to choose a design co-ordinator to manage the design process. Ultimately he would then be responsible for hiring the team of designers and would be in charge of that side of the programme. All major design decisions would be justified, explained and well considered by the wider team – in particular by the sailing team who were set up as the clients. America³ was the first team to adopt the philosophy of hiring a design co-ordinator who was a scientist rather than a naval architect to lead the design programme. Team New Zealand took it another step by requiring this design co-ordinator to also sail on the race boat to enhance communication between the sailors and designers.

Tom Schnackenberg was the logical choice to co-ordinate the design process. He brought a wealth of experience with him having campaigned in many previous Cups with the Australians, including the record-shattering win of *Australia II* in 1983. A nuclear physicist by trade, Schnackenberg became one of the principal designers of modern computer software for North Sails throughout the 1970s and '80s. Although not a recognised hull designer, he had the technical ability to understand the big picture and to co-ordinate the scientific testing as well as sail on the race boat as navigator. The designers and sailors respected his ability, and the cost versus rewards for all the design projects were always well debated and well researched. Much of the credit for the overall programme running within budget should be credited to Schnackenberg's management and analytical methods which identified the most cost-effective areas to provide the biggest gains.

Laurie Davidson and Doug Peterson were hired as the principal hull designers. Peterson was lured from the successful America³ team in an effort to bridge the gap in technical knowledge. Davidson's intuitive style earned him considerable respect in previous campaigns such as New

Design team leader Tom Schnackenberg (left) and meteorologist Bob Rice played key roles in the Team New Zealand victory.

The partnership of helmsman Russell Coutts (right) and tactician Brad Butterworth has proved successful not only in America's Cup racing, but also on the international match racing circuit and in many of the world's most prestigious fleet races.

New Zealander Laurie Davidson (below) and American Doug Peterson (left) were the principal hull designers in 1995. Both were veterans of America's Cups past and Davidson will play a key role for Team New Zealand in the 2000 event. Peterson is now working for the Italian *Prada* team.

NEW ZEALAND

Zealand's first challenge in 1986/87 and he would prove to be a central figure in the hull design process. Aerodynamicist Richard Karn, also known to the group through his development of the keel for *KZ-7* in that original campaign, was retained to work on the appendage and spar programme. David Egan, who had been working for McDonald Douglas, was brought in to develop CFD (computational fluid design) computer codes for appendage, sail and hull design.

Steve Wilson, an owner of Southern Spars, had responsibility for the rig design. He combined with Richard Karn and structural and composite engineer Chris Mitchell, formerly with *Il Moro Di Venezia* in 1992, to develop a mast that was later regarded as one of the most significant performance advantages that *Black Magic* enjoyed in San Diego. Mike Drummond, Wayne Smith and Neil Wilkinson were responsible for the material testing, structural analysis and design of the hull and components.

The sailing team were selected by Coutts with many significant changes from the previous teams. Only two crew members from 1992, grinder Andrew Taylor and trimmer Simon Daubney, retained their primary roles for 1995. With the America's Cup having a strong focus on technology, a lot of weight was given to proven ability in secondary functions. Many of the multi-skilled Whitbread Round the World sailors were chosen including Brad Butterworth, Dean Phipps, Joe Allen, Matthew Mason, Ross Halcrow, Robbie Naismith and Tony Rae.

From the Olympic yachting stable came Murray Jones, Richard Dodson and Craig Monk. Their non-selection for previous America's Cup efforts seemed an oversight when their talents were considered. As a four-time Olympic qualifier, Jones is one of the most successful and innovative small-boat helmsmen in the country. He is co-owner of Matrix spar making company and worked closely with Steve Wilson to develop the spar and rigging concepts. Monk is a qualified sailmaker, and has won a bronze medal as a helmsman and yet had a principal role as grinder. Dodson is a part owner of North Sails and was highly respected by Coutts as a tactician from previous Olympic Finn Class days. Dodson was also a successful big-boat helmsman in his own right, winning the Admirals Cup in 1987 and the One Ton Cup in 1988.

Coutts had also combined well with Nick Heron, Warwick Fleury, Jeremy Scantlebury, Mike Drummond and Tom Schnackenberg on various occasions to win match-racing events culminating in the match-racing world championships in 1992 and 1993.

Blake used his previous Whitbread experience to hire Tim Gurr to head the boatbuilding side of the operation. Gurr assembled a highly skilled team of boatbuilders who produced two of the fastest IACC yachts while also perfectly maintaining them throughout the campaign at San Diego. There were no serious breakdowns during racing that prevented the black boats from winning. Bob Rice was brought in from the United States to run the weather programme, which was considered to be the best in San Diego.

Motivation within the team was very high. Although there were many new faces, there was a sense that this would be the last New Zealand challenge if it was unsuccessful. In many ways, the new faces proved to be an advantage. It was easier to develop a new culture in which team members were sharing ideas and looking for self-improvement and self-evaluation. All of the major decisions were team decisions and therefore the justification for those decisions was well understood. There was no room for complacency because two of the previous New Zealand teams were beaten right at the very end of their respective challenger series. While the team were confident, the overwhelming success on the race course in 1995 was something that nobody within the team would have predicted. The goal was also simple in that the whole team were focussed on winning and achieving what no other New Zealand team had done before.

Defending the Cup in 2000 represents a different proposition to winning it for the first time. Before *Australia II*'s victory in 1983, the Americans had successfully defended the Cup for 132 years. Since 1983 however, the Cup has been won by the challengers three times and yet successfully defended only twice (one time being the big boat/catamaran mismatch). America is

Above: Richard Dodson, an important member of the afterguard team.

Right: Tony Rae, who with Warwick Fleury has co-ordinated the mainsail development.

Below left: Richard Karn from Napier works on the aero/hydrodynamics of the mast, keel and rudder.

Below middle: Tim Gurr manages the shore team and boatbuilding operations.

Below right: Steve Wilson from Southern Spars has co-ordinated the mast programme.

the only nation to ever successfully defend the Cup. The swing in advantage is due to changes in the rules, allowing more widespread use of technology, as well as the sheer number of challengers versus defender. For 2000, 13 challengers are expected to participate so the challenging group is exposed to a wider spread of ideas. They will also have the benefit of being able to race each other in order to gauge their respective performance. On February 19, 2000, Team New Zealand will line up against the best challenger and only then will they be able to gauge their performance versus the rest of the world.

Defending the Cup may well prove to be more difficult than winning it. Traditionally, defenders in sport are overly defensive and conservative in both their approach and execution. Realising the odds may be stacked against the defender, Team New Zealand 2000 may better be served believing they are trying to win the Cup rather than trying to defend it!

When one of the experienced members of the Australian defence for 1987 was asked about their failure he responded, "Complacency was one of the key reasons we lost." The team were not chasing new ideas and improvement with the same passion, and new team members did not receive the same stature as those who were involved in 1983. The old ways prevailed and although they were good enough in 1983, better thinking in 1987 eclipsed them. After such a dominant performance in 1995, the tendency to assume that the principles applied last time will work again could be a real danger. The team have also matured in the five-year gap and personal goals may have changed. The individual roles will have to reflect these changes.

One of the key advantages for Team New Zealand is that the core group of sponsorship partners has been retained. New Zealand Lotteries, Steinlager, Toyota and Television New Zealand's One network are all back. With such a strong family of sponsors, it was easy to persuade Telecom also to join, meaning that funding for design and research was available from a very early stage. With this funding secured, much of the successful team from 1995 was able to be retained. On the surface, retaining the same knowledge and skill from last time should be an advantage. However, if 1995 represented the best ideas the team had, developing new ideas may be more difficult. One of the challenges Team New Zealand faced after the success of 1995 was to bring the game to yet another new level. The performance achieved last time will not be adequate five years later. Advances in technology, thinking and management should mean the new America's Cup is contested at an even higher level.

How then have Team New Zealand changed since 1995? One of the most significant changes was that Doug Peterson and David Egan moved to the Italian camp, joining the Prada-sponsored syndicate. Team New Zealand replaced Peterson with Clay Oliver, who was involved with Dennis Conner's Stars & Stripes syndicate in its successful 1987 win. Oliver also played a pivotal role in Team New Zealand's 1995 victory as he designed the VPP (Velocity Prediction Program) to measure performance. It was felt that not only could Oliver improve the accuracy of the VPP, but he would also bring new expertise and ideas for hull design.

A key focus for Team New Zealand was to improve the understanding of why certain components were behaving as they were in 1995 and to progress towards better refinement of those components. Having access to Clay Oliver full-time will no doubt improve the level of scientific knowledge within the group. Nick Holroyd was also hired to assist with performance prediction and run the various CFD (Computational Fluid Dynamics) codes that the team are now using.

Over the past three summers the team have been testing full-size yachts on Auckland's Waitemata Harbour, Mike Drummond has played a more dominant role in managing the on-the-water test programme. In fact, most of the design team have played an active role on the water both to gain a first-hand understanding of the results and to increase communication between the sailing and design teams. Again the focus has been on rationalising the reasons behind the various differences in performance to allow more accuracy for the final design. One of the larger features tested was the precise relationship between sail area versus waterline

Simon Daubney (left), Dean Phipps (foreground) and Craig Monk at work during another day at the office.

Andrew Taylor (left) and Craig Monk provide the muscle to the winches that trim the sails.

Murray Jones was usually at the helm of one of the black boats with Coutts or Dean Barker at the other during team training exercises and boatspeed testing.

One of New Zealand's brightest new helmsmen, Dean Barker, assisted by experienced sail trimmer Grant Loretz in the foreground.

Above: James Dagg is one of the new trimmers who has gained an international reputation since joining Team New Zealand.

Left: Robbie Naismith, known as "The Battler" for his fierce competitive spirit, was the starboard trimmer during the 1995 Cup and will return for the defence in 2000.

Barry McKay (above) will see action on Waitemata Harbour when Team New Zealand defends. He'll be joined by weather analyst Peter Evans and new bowman Matt Mitchell (right).

Steinlager

TVNZ

Telecom

Telecom
NEW ZEALAND
Steinlager
ON
LOTTO

TOYOTA   Telecom   LOTTO   one   Steinlager

NEW ZEALAND

The crew were keen to put *NZL-57* through her paces from the first trials. Early indications were promising.

length as related to the America's Cup Rule. As sail area is reduced, waterline length can be increased which will produce a boat that will be better in stronger winds. The amount of sail area selected will prove to be a key point in configuring the defending yacht against what the team perceive to be the performance of the best challenging yacht.

Another key feature tested was bow shapes. During 1997, the metre bow of *NZL-38* was replaced with a destroyer-type bow to test the effect in the different sea conditions of Auckland. The previous year, *NZL-38* had her mast position moved forward to test the effects of balance with less angle on the rudder in stronger winds. Material and structural testing has also been a big factor in Team New Zealand's testing. The windier conditions have meant a significant shift in mindset from San Diego where yachts competed in almost all races in under 20 knots of wind. Measuring the precise loads on rigging should mean the final yacht can be built close to the minimum weight possible without risking failure.

In San Diego, Team New Zealand's weather programme was widely regarded as one of the major strengths of the tactical team. Bob Rice and Mike Drummond worked with uncanny accuracy to determine which side of the course would be favoured on the first leg. The sailing team became supremely confident in their predictions and began to rely on their decisions without question. Auckland's shifting conditions may make this part of the programme even more vital. Peter Evans, who was a tactician for Nippon challenge in 1995 and has also won the match-racing worlds as a tactician with Coutts, was hired in to work with Rice. Evans brings a fundamental knowledge of the racing area having sailed almost his entire career on the waters of the racecourse. He has won two Olympic trials in the same waters and is reported to have brought the weather programme to a new level.

The sailing team have been boosted in numbers with eleven new sailors joining the team while only two sailors moved to competing camps after 1995. Coutts and the team were quick to seize this opportunity to bring in new talent. Grant Loretz was hired to assist with the sail

From left to right: Jeremy Scantlebury, the pitman in 1995, will sail again in 2000. With Matthew Mason and Barry McKay, he has had a key role in developing the hardware systems for the new boats. Chris Mitchell worked on the structural analysis of the new masts. Large cord wing masts were tested early in '99 and are seen as one of the key developments for 2000. Matthew Mason was mastman in 1995. He has co-ordinated the deck system for the current campaign. Mike Drummond has established a lead role in the design group, analysing the trade-off between various new and old concepts.

Chris Ward working out during the team's daily fitness routine.

Joe Allen: his experience and humour will be an invaluable asset for the team.

Hamish Pepper has made the transition from small boats to the America's Cup Class. He has been combining well as tactician for Dean Barker on the match racing circuit.

Clay Oliver, one of the principal designers for Team New Zealand. His new and creative ideas were a major bonus for the team.

programme and Barry McKay was moved into the sailing programme. Former kayak specialist John MacBeth, after being tested and trained as a grinder for 12 months, was also given a full-time role. Loretz crewed on Chris Dickson's America's Cup contender *Tag Heuer* in 1995 and was with New Zealand Challenge in 1992 as a primary sail trimmer. He is a skilled and respected sail designer and brings a wealth of experience along with some new thinking to the sail programme. McKay was also involved in New Zealand's 1992 effort and was brought into the boatbuilding programme late in 1995 after crewing with Peter Blake on the 90ft catamaran *ENZA*, in their successful Jules Verne Round the World record attempt. Peter Waymouth, who worked with McKay on the yacht *Morning Glory* and also with Steve Wilson on *Southern Spars*, has been added to the sailing team for his multi-skilled ability.

Realising that there will not be the same variety of competition that the challengers will enjoy during the Louis Vuitton Cup, the team have set about increasing the level of skill throughout the group. The target is to produce at least two equal crews, each capable of winning the America's Cup, resulting in a better standard of internal competition and suitable back-ups for all crew positions. At times there have been at least four Team New Zealand teams competing around the world in match-racing events as well as ocean races, IMS Maxis, 50 footers, world championships and Admirals Cups.

One of the features of the current team is the extent of depth and experience. In 1996 Coutts and his Team Magic crew had one of their most successful years ever, dominating every Brut sailing series event and the world championship. They have since been unable to repeat that form although they have not been regular attendees on the match-racing circuit, choosing instead to concentrate on other events. When Team Magic is present, it is a force to be reckoned with as it did not finish outside of the top two in 1997 and 1998. It should also be noted that Coutts and the majority of the Team Magic crew have won the last three match-racing world championships they have competed in – in 1992, 1993 and 1996. The fact that Butterworth, Coutts, Daubney, Fleury and Phipps compete so regularly together should be an advantage for the larger team. Butterworth's involvement in the America's Cup since 1983 is a key advantage in balancing the rules issues and associated politics that can often be a disruptive factor for any team.

The 26-year-old Dean Barker, and his primarily younger team, have also shown tremendous promise on the match-racing circuit, putting together a string of first and second finishes. He has joined test helmsman Murray Jones, who has also enjoyed some high finishes in 1997 and 1998, as a viable back-up for Coutts. Barker is working well with Olympic Laser representative Hamish Pepper and this combination could well be being groomed for future America's Cup competition. It has been a focus of Team New Zealand to invest in the future, with most of the new sailors being under the age of 26. James Dagg, Matt Mitchell, Cameron Appleton and Mathew Hughes will have key roles to play in the future. Jared Henderson, having completed a successful Whitbread campaign with Grant Dalton on *Merit Cup*, has also been added to the sailing team with the future in mind.

With the conditions in Auckland being more challenging, racing a 75ft yacht with a crew of 16 people will demand a significantly higher level of fitness than was required in San Diego. The possibility of using a slightly different crew for stronger winds has not been missed and it is notable that Dennis Conner used crew substitutions in Fremantle while the Kiwis stuck with the same crew for all races. It may be expected that Team New Zealand will stack their race boat with bigger and stronger sailors for conditions of 20 knots or more.

The question is still being debated as to whether Team New Zealand will be battle-hardened on 19 February 2000. The challengers individually may race more than 70 races before the best yacht and team are selected. Only time will tell when the final result is known. However, as Paul Cayard has remarked: "One thing is certain. The defender in 2000 will not be as far off the pace as the defenders were in 1995."

CHAPTER 6

The Challengers

The quest to win America's Cup 2000 began, in many respects, minutes after Team New Zealand's *Black Magic* crossed the finish line ahead of *Young America* on May 13, 1995. As the fifth and deciding race of the 29th Cup became history and it was recognised that the next contest would be played out on New Zealand waters, the first order of business was for the new defender to be challenged. Tradition, or at least a loose sense of history, dictated that the wheels of Cup organisation do not begin to turn until an official challenge is proffered and accepted.

Officially, any yacht club based anywhere in the world can challenge the defender as long as the yacht club meets the criteria as set out in the Deed of Gift. It is the defender's responsibility to select a "Challenger of Record", the designation given to the club which will then serve as a sort of clearing house for all the challengers and the procedural issues and questions that inevitably arise. The club also has the responsibility of running the challenger selection trials, no easy feat.

The process of selecting a Challenger of Record has changed through the years. When the New York Yacht Club had firm control of the Cup for some 132 years, challenges were received and accepted in all manner and at many different times. In the early days of the America's Cup, the club sometimes waited for several years before a challenger came forward. In other years, especially during the 12-metre era, lines quickly formed when the final race of a Cup series was in sight. Selection as the Challenger of Record gave certain benefits to the challenger, chief of which is supposedly an "equal" voice to the defender's in determining such things as racing ground rules and the actual dates of racing.

For their part, the defender (in almost 150 years of Cup racing there have been only four) looks to choose a challenging club somewhat *simpatico* with the overall vision they have. This has led to the establishment of what is known as the "hip-pocket" challenge, a pre-determined arrangement between the club which appears to be the next defender and a club that has resolved to become an official challenger. This is necessary to subvert the idea that the Challenger of Record be automatically assigned to the club that puts forth the first challenge. Because there was not a multi-club challenge until 1970, the need for a pre-arrangement never arose. But as more nations and more sailors entered the game over the past three decades, the hip-pocket challenge has become utilised more frequently.

In 1995, as Team New Zealand's Black Boats battered the opposition race after race, it became clear it would take a superior effort by the defender to keep the Cup on American shores. And long before that defender was even known, it also became clear that the likelihood of a superior effort was minimal at best. Thus, the backroom lobbying began during the Louis Vuitton Cup and intensified with each Team New Zealand win in the America's Cup.

Bill Koch prided himself on being equal to the political and rule-bending shenanigans that have become part of the event. In 1992 he had battled the San Diego Yacht Club to at least a draw in his effort to become the defender over hometown favourite and former SDYC commodore Dennis Conner. In 1995 he brought an all-women's team into the fray, an act for which many more traditionally minded yachtsmen may never forgive him. He had stood up to the yachting establishment time and time again and his record proved he had won more times than he had lost.

But Koch, who focused his attention on the Challenger of Record title once his women's team had been eliminated by arch-rival Conner, was a novice in the game compared to the guys who invented the game – the New York Yacht Club. Since the Cup had left their hallowed halls in 1983, the New Yorkers had participated in only one contest as a challenger. That ended quickly with an early exit in the Fremantle competition and as members' enthusiasm dampened and campaign expenses escalated, the club chose to sit out the past three America's Cups.

Sitting on the sidelines hurt even more. To many members, the America's Cup and the New York Yacht Club were a partnership forged in history and cemented through 132 years of battle. Although many of their countrymen believed the Australians' 1983 victory was the best thing that ever happened to the event, there were still a good number of members who didn't agree. They wanted the Cup back where they believed it belonged. And to get it back, they would have to back a challenge. Exactly when this was decided is lost to history, but there is clear evidence that it had been determined that the club would re-enter the game after the 1995 event and that those members involved wanted the title of Challenger of Record as well.

Koch never had a chance. Although he had laid the groundwork and was accompanied by the commodore of his yacht club in Osterville, Massachusetts, and his inflatable was the first to reach Team New Zealand, the New Yorkers' hip-pocket challenge had already been delivered to the Royal New Zealand Yacht Squadron. Sir Peter Blake, head of Team New Zealand, announced at the final press conference that his team had received and accepted the challenge from the New York Yacht Club, confirming a rumour that had spread through San Diego for days. The club had its challenge; now all it needed was a challenger.

Four options presented themselves. The three 1995 defence candidates (Koch's America[3], Conner's Stars & Stripes and John Marshall's PACT '95) had viable syndicates already formed. The New Yorkers could join forces with one of them or begin from scratch with their own organisation. Negotiations began, the talks were lengthy and in the end the club decided to affiliate with Marshall and his group. Conner, now used to finding his own way when the New York Yacht Club looked elsewhere for a skipper, launched his challenge through the Cortez Racing Association in San Diego. Koch, who once vowed he would never become involved in America's Cup racing because of the strain it puts on friendships, stepped to the sidelines so recently vacated by the New Yorkers.

Blake also announced at the final press briefing that the next Cup would be held in the year 2000, with challenger races beginning at the end of 1999. Why so long? After all, the past four events had been held in '86, '88, '92 and '95. Blake's answer was based on practicality. Many of the sailors who would race in Auckland were the same individuals who were already committed to be on board for the final Whitbread Round the World Race in 1997/98 (it is now called the Volvo Ocean Race). His second reason, even more compelling, was that Auckland simply did not have the infrastructure to deal with a six-month America's Cup programme. It would take time to raise the money needed to dredge the harbour, build the Cup village envisioned by the Kiwis and adequately prepare for the expected invasion of international teams.

There was another reason that the year 2000 had a magical ring to New Zealanders. Across the Tasman Sea in Sydney, Australians were already preparing for an invasion of their own – the Olympic Games. Rivals in so many sporting contests through the years, Aussies and Kiwis

The variety of design amongst the challenging boats should provide for a very interesting competition in Auckland's changeable wind conditions. Here *AmericaOne* shows her lines during a test trial off Long Beach, California.

never tire of competing against each other on and off the athletic field. Here was one more chance for New Zealand to perhaps steal a little of the thunder away from the larger nation, while at the same time informally partnering with Australia to invite the world Down Under to begin the new millennium.

Although Cup enthusiasts might have wished for an earlier start to the action, challengers around the world knew that fundraising schedules could use every hour given to them. As has been said many times, the real race for the America's Cup is often won on land even before boats are built and that race is the race for money. Budgets are ever increasing. Sailors, materials, technology, equipment, housing, food, all cost more today than they did five and six years ago. The sooner the funds are raised, the sooner the entire scope of a challenger's programme can be initiated. Teams with money in the bank can spend their time developing the sailing and construction and technology operations while those still looking for funds spend their time, well, looking for funds.

By the time the 1995 contenders had packed their gear, sold or stored their equipment and left San Diego to resume their pre-America's Cup lives, talk of the 2000 event was beginning to drift through yacht clubs around the world. The new venue presented an exciting challenge to sailors. Winds and conditions in the Hauraki Gulf were unpredictable. The class of boats to be raced would be the same as in California, but designers recognised immediately that what worked in the prevailing light winds off San Diego most likely would not stand up to six months of varying extremes off Auckland.

One of the first announcements regarding the next Cup came from Team New Zealand which made it clear that they would be the only defence team. There were a number of reasons for this declaration, most of which had to do with the limited resources of the small island nation. Although Chris Dickson and his Tag Heuer team had performed surprisingly well in 1995 as a New Zealand challenger on a shoestring budget, the powers that be in Team New Zealand reasoned that a one-team, concentrated defence effort was the best utilisation of the nation's sailing talent and budget. Considering the millions that were to be spent on improving the infrastructure and running the event, not to mention the dollars needed to fund the defence, it was quickly understood there was just so much to go around.

With the defender announced, the focus in the sailing world turned to potential challengers. By January 31, 1998, 16 teams from 10 nations had deposited $US250,000 each to officially declare themselves in the hunt for, first, the Louis Vuitton Cup and then, if luck and skill held out, for the America's Cup. Louis Vuitton, the prestigious French company known for luxury goods, particularly luggage, began sponsoring the challenger selection trials in 1983. The America's Cup event has benefited greatly not only from the sponsorship dollars, but also from the organisation of the races and from the knowledgeable personnel and state-of-the-art technology employed by the media centre the company also sponsors to keep the world informed of racing results.

While 16 teams met the criteria to be named as official challengers, not all of them will make it to the starting line. Already the team from the US Virgin Islands has found the fundraising hurdle too great to overcome and have "merged" with Team Dennis Conner. Hong Kong and the United Kingdom dropped out, but Russia and the merged French team called Le Defi Sud maintain they will be on the starting line in Auckland. But there are still enough viable challengers with plans to be on the starting line to make the 1999/2000 Louis Vuitton Cup the most populated contest since 13 syndicates challenged in 1986/87. Some (with money) plan two-boat campaigns, some (who found fundraising more difficult) will head to Auckland with one new boat. The outcome, as always, will be determined by design and sailing skills, and no small measure of luck.

ITALY

ITA45
ITA48

Luna Rossa

Fact File

Sponsors	Prada	Helmsman	Francesco de Angelis
Yacht Name	*Luna Rossa*	Tactician	Torben Grael
Sail Number	ITA-45, ITA-48	Navigator	Matteo Plazzi
Designers	Frers, Peterson, Egan	Others	Rod Davis

It seems that every docksider's early pick for the Louis Vuitton Cup is the Prada-sponsored two-boat team from Italy. One of the first challengers to be formed, the team boast the dream set-up – a single sponsor who takes care of the bills while all other aspects of the campaign can be carried out with singular concentration. That fact alone puts the design, construction and sailing operations perhaps as much as a year to 18 months ahead of all other challengers, with the possible exception of the New York Yacht Club's Young America.

But money isn't Italy's only advantage. The design team are overflowing with talent, skill and proven America's Cup experience. Argentinean German Frers' list of winning ocean-racing designs earned him a ticket to Milan to draw lines for the 1992 Il Moro di Venezia syndicate. The boat he and his team designed beat all challengers and took Italy into the America's Cup match for the first time in history. Although the trophy went to Bill Koch and his America[3] group, the *Il Moro* performance was strong enough to warrant a recall of Frers by Prada.

Cup historians will remember that Frers was at the centre of a residency controversy concerning two American syndicates in 1986. After two boats had been designed and built to the disappointment of some members of the New York Yacht Club, a faction within the club began an intense lobbying campaign to bring in Frers to design another boat. Another faction, led by skipper John Kolius, stood steadfast behind their designer. The debate turned somewhat bitter and led to a change in management which resulted in the temporary resignation of Kolius, another management shake-up and the skipper's eventual return.

If the Frers issue was the catalyst to management musical chairs in New York, his appointment as designer of the Buddy Melges-led Heart of America campaign out of Chicago helped solidify that effort. But alas, only temporarily, before his eligibility was questioned and deemed not sufficient to allow his employment. It was a lesson well learned by both the Il Moro and Prada teams, which arranged the designer's Italian residency in plenty of time to comply with Cup rules.

For the 2000 contest, the residency requirement was also met by the American designer Doug Peterson who brings an impressive Cup history to the design table. An integral part of the design team that drew 1992 winner *America[3]*, Peterson was then hired by Team New Zealand for the 1995 campaign. He shared the responsibility of creating the hull lines and the overall design concept of the black boats with Laurie Davidson.

Team New Zealand also lost David Egan to Prada. Egan is responsible for computational codes and computer modelling. In Auckland he worked on appendages and concentrated on the hydrodynamics of the keel, its stem and its wings as well as the aerodynamics of the rig.

Filling out the Prada design team are German Frers Jr and Guido Cavalazzi. Frers

Jr oversees the tank test work outside of Rome and Cavalazzi's major responsibility is the design of the sails.

As more personnel were added, the team began to take on the complexion of a mini United Nations at sea. Heading operations is Frenchman Laurent Esquier. Sailing coach is Rod Davis, born in America and living in New Zealand, who last raced with *oneAustralia*. Tactician Torben Grael is from Brazil. The syndicate did go home to select their helmsman, Francesco de Angelis, who has earned a reputation as one of the premier skippers in Europe. After his name was added to the roster, the first order of business for de Angelis was to gain match-racing experience.

"I have not competed in match races before," said the tall, soft-spoken Italian at the 1997 Virgin Islands International Match Race in St Thomas. "This is the first match-race regatta I've participated in as a helmsman. Between now and the America's Cup, we will try to be invited to as many match races as possible. I need to learn the particulars of this type of racing."

His advancement to the semi-finals of the Virgin Islands' contest illustrated his skill at the wheel and his ability to learn quickly. But his uneven record since then speaks to the ever-increasing competition on the international match-racing circuit, known as the "training ground for the America's Cup". Time and time again de Angelis and his match racing team, which includes Grael, a highly rated helmsman in his own right, raced against teams that will be competing in Auckland. How much experience was gained and how sharply the skills were tuned will become evident on the Hauraki Gulf.

While match racing may not be his forte, de Angelis' record in fleet racing is enviable. With roots in the Finn class, he held a number of Italian, European and World titles in the J24, Star and One Ton Classes during the 1980s. In 1988 he took charge of the BRAVA team, a campaign that culminated in an Admiral's Cup win in 1995. At the helm was de Angelis.

Few sailors racing today can duplicate Torben Grael's record. Most recently he won the Olympic gold medal in the extremely competitive Star Class at the 1996 Games in

The new yachts from Prada being tested in early trials off Punta Ala, Italy.

Brazillian Torben Grael, Olympic gold medal winner in the Star class, will call tactics for Team Prada.

Doug Peterson brings his experience as part of the design teams that created '92 winner *America³* and '95 victor *Black Magic* to the Italian team for 1999/2000.

Francesco de Angelis was selected as Prada's helmsman in 1996 and has devoted considerable time since then to the intricacies of match racing, the one-on-one format used in the America's Cup.

Prada's compound in Auckland was home to two yachts acquired from Bill Koch's *America³* syndicate when the team trained in New Zealand. The compound is said to be one of the largest and most lavish sites in the America's Cup Village.

Prada's sailing coach, Rod Davis, includes Olympic, America's Cup and match racing experience on his resume. In Cup action, he has served as crew, coach and helmsman.

Atlanta. He won a bronze medal in the same class at Seoul in 1988 and a silver medal in the Soling Class in 1984 at Los Angeles. He holds five One Ton world champion titles and has travelled the match-race circuit as tactician over the past two years with de Angelis.

Prada's sailing coach is Davis, one of the most experienced match-racing and America's Cup sailors in the world. Originally from San Diego, Davis is the grandson of an admiral and the son of a submarine commander. He first appeared in Cup

competition at age 21 as bowman aboard *Enterprise* in the 1977 defender trials. He coached the Australian challenge in 1980. In 1983 he sailed on *Defender*, again in the defence trials, and then was named helmsman of *Eagle* in the 1986/87 Cup as a challenger. In 1992 he skippered *New Zealand* in all but two races and three years later he was at the wheel of *oneAustralia*. Add to that Olympic gold (1984, Soling) and silver (1992, Star) medals, plus considerable professional match-racing experience (and many victories), and it is not difficult to understand why Prada hired him.

Also bringing considerable depth of Cup experience is Laurent Esquier. As operations manager, he has similar responsibilities to those he had in 1992 for the Il Moro di Venezia syndicate. He also knows New Zealand waters from his time as coach and operations manager with the first Kiwi challenge in 1986/87 and the "Big Boat" campaign in 1988. Esquier also crewed on the French teams in 1974 and 1977.

The president and CEO of the Prada challenge is Patrizio Bertelli, husband of Miuccia Prada, granddaughter of the founder of the well-known fashion house. Bertelli has made it clear that the company's sponsorship is not to be mistaken as solely an advertisement for its products. He is a fierce competitor in both sailing (he owns the 1937 Olin Stephens designed 12-metre *Nyala*) and business and he has transferred that energy and spirit to the America's Cup. "We are doing the America's Cup to win the America's Cup," he has said.

~ Russell Coutts

Prada is definitely one of the favourites to reach the challenger finals. The team have enjoyed the advantage of a large budget from the start of their programme.

Their design team looks very strong and full of experience, with Doug Peterson and David Egan coming from Team New Zealand and German Frers' experience with Il Moro.

The sailing team are very capable and are made up of champions. Their lack of experience in match racing could be their only weakness, although they have been working very hard in this area and should surprise many teams with better tactics.

Italy can still draw upon the experience gained in 1992 when they put together a campaign that almost won. The 1999/2000 campaign has some of the same key players. They have spent two full summers in Auckland while also sailing the summer seasons in Italy, practising and testing almost full time from 1997. They deserve to be rated as very tough.

The second new boat, *Luna Rossa*, sailing upwind.

NIPPON

JPN44
JPN52

NCBT

Fact File

Sponsors	Nu Skin, Casio, KDD, Sumitomo Marine & Fire Insurance, Daidoh, Tokyo News Service, Toyota, Nissui, Yamaha, S&B, Omron, Sunkusu, Mitsubishi Rayon, Asahi Breweries, JAL, Hewlett Packard, Pizza-La, Ajinomoto, Ozeki	Yacht Name	*NCBT*
		Sail Number	JPN-44, JPN-52
		Designers	Hideaki Miyata & ACtech
		Helmsman	Peter Gilmour
		Afterguard	Makoto Kikuchi, Masanobu Katori, Tatsu Wakinaga, Kazuyuki Hyodo

As one of the world's leading industrial and technological powers, it is somewhat surprising that Japan, an island nation, did not enter the America's Cup arena before 1992. It isn't that the sport of sailboat racing was unknown there, just that it wasn't widely practised. The force behind Japan's Cup efforts has been Tatsumitsu Yamasaki, chairman of S&B foods, Asia's market leader in the importation of spices. When a challenge was first conceived some five years before the '92 event, Japan had no Cup infrastructure on which to build: no boats, no sailors with Cup experience, no Cup-specific technology.

Yamasaki must have thought, "If they can do it, why can't we?" To solve his no-boat problem he purchased the first two fibreglass 12-metres built by New Zealand and hired four Kiwis to form the core of Japan's first effort: Chris Dickson as skipper, John Cutler as tactician, Erle Williams who had raced on *KZ-7* in Fremantle, and Mike Spanhake, a sailmaker and trimmer. It was Dickson's responsibility, having just led his countrymen to an outstanding performance in Australia, to train the Japanese. It was an immense undertaking given the little knowledge of sailing possessed by most of the crew.

The Nippon challenge made its debut in big league sailing in 1991 at the International America's Cup Class (IACC) World Championships. It was less than successful. The two 12-metres which had been intended as training platforms were deemed irrelevant when the IACC formula was adopted in answer to the Big Boat/Catamaran debacle of 1988. On board the bigger, faster and some say more dangerous racing yachts, the new team never gained their poise. One race ended with a man overboard. Blown-out sails and gear breakage were all-too-frequent occurrences and when a half-million-dollar carbon fibre mast snapped and fell to the deck, the team lost more than just face.

But neither Yamasaki, Dickson, the Kiwis, or the Japanese crew gave up and they came out of the Louis Vuitton Cup round robin as points leader before falling in the semi-finals.

The '92 effort was encouraging and Yamasaki quickly joined the challengers for the 1995 contest. An emphasis on technology was behind a restructuring of the design and technical teams, with more Japanese recruited. Dickson left and formed the Tutukaka challenge in New Zealand while Cutler took his place behind the Nippon wheel. Match-racing

Peter Gilmour steers one of the new Nippon boats in early sea trials off Gamagori.

star Makoto Namba came on board and was named skipper just before the challenger trials began and Australian Peter Gilmour joined as coach and helmsman of the trial boat.

The team were the first to launch a new IACC boat, *JPN-30*, for the '95 event. The boat was tested against the '92 racer for almost a year before the final yacht was built. The Nippon challenge once again advanced to the Louis Vuitton Cup semi-finals, but the quantum leap in boatspeed hoped for in the new yacht was not there. The rebuilt *JPN-30* sailed to a 9-9 record before *JPN-41* squeaked into the semis with a 2-4 record. The team lost all 11 races in the semi-finals.

Once the disappointment subsided, Yamasaki and his avid followers looked to

their accomplishments. Where there had been no boats, no experience, no America's Cup infrastructure just a decade before, there was now a bona fide Cup community that counts as its assets five IACC yachts, 13 years of design knowledge, sailors who have been tested in intense competition, and a strong core of sponsorship support.

As chairman Yamasaki reviewed these assets, his thoughts must have focused on the New Zealand victory in San Diego. Less than 10 years had passed since the Kiwis first joined the Cup fray and now they won the right to host the event.

So for the third consecutive America's Cup, Japan will challenge again. But soon after the announcement, Nippon was rocked by two events. Makoto Namba was lost at sea when a rogue wave washed him

The two new Nippon boats testing in Japan.

Engineering at the University of Tokyo.

The committee has relied heavily on computer modelling and CFD (computational fluid dynamics) tools to create some 50 designs which, after testing, evolved into five models which have been tank tested. The Nippon team seem confident that their yacht development, combined with considerable research conducted on the wind and wave conditions on the Auckland race course, will produce an advanced racing yacht.

Who will steer and crew the yacht was resolved shortly after the '95 team returned to Japan from San Diego. Chairman Yamasaki recognised the qualities Peter Gilmour brought to the Nippon programme both on and off the water by naming him skipper and helmsman for the new campaign. The decision was met with approval by team veterans who appreciate the Australian's skills and talents. For almost as long as Japan has been involved in the America's Cup, Gilmour has been listed among the top five ranked match-racing sailors in the world, often reaching number one. As sailing coach of Nippon and skipper of the trial horse in 1995, his contributions were significant.

While funding hasn't allowed a concentrated crew training effort, Gilmour formed a core team of challenge sailors several years ago that has been a regular competitor on the international match-racing circuit. Sponsored by Pizza-La, the team have often raced their way into regatta finals and have emerged champions in a number of tightly contested battles. In 1997 Gilmour and crew won the World Championship of Match Race Sailing and also achieved the number-one ranking, a position familiar to the skipper.

Nippon has launched two new boats, *JPN-44* and *JPN-52*. The fact that the Nippon challenge has persevered through what has to be its darkest days to achieve a two-boat programme is testament to the syndicate's strength. Having reached the semi-finals of the Louis Vuitton Cup in its previous two

overboard during a race off Japan's coast. The other setback was shared by financial markets throughout the world. When Japan's economy faltered, sparking the Asian economic crisis, the challenge's fundraising efforts were severely crippled. Unlike the previous two campaigns that were up and running at full speed as many as three years in advance of racing, Nippon 1999/2000 will forgo many preliminary training exercises in deference to a leaner budget. But the emphasis on technology, a mainstay of Nippon '92 and '95, remains intact.

The approach to design has been altered somewhat with a committee being formed and given the responsibility of designing and building two new IACC boats and the design process has been under way since the spring of 1996. Co-ordinating the efforts is Professor Hideaki Miyata from the Department of Naval Architecture and Ocean

attempts, Nippon presents a strong case as a potential finalist in Auckland.

~ Russell Coutts

They were quick to hire the talents of former world match-racing champion Peter Gilmour from Australia who has since moulded the Japanese team into a very strong unit. They have competed against and beaten most of the top America's Cup teams in various match and fleet-racing events around the world, earning the utmost respect of all the competing sailors.

The team have been preparing quietly, including sailing their old boats in Japan and saying almost nothing publicly. They have built two new boats and appear to have all the resources necessary to win.

This team may be the strongest Japanese entry in the America's Cup to date.

Skipper of the Nippon challenge for 1999/2000 is Australian Peter Gilmour, ranked among the top five match racers in the world for more than a decade.

Makoto Namba, who led the Japanese challenge in 1995, tragically died after being washed overboard during an offshore race. His immense contribution will be missed in 2000.

Peter Gilmour has been sailing with an all-Japanese team on the international match racing circuit for several years as part of Team Brut and then under the auspices of sponsor Pizza-La.

Nippon base camp in Gamagori and the launching of Nippon's two new boats. Nippon has received great support from the city which recognises the huge benefits should Nippon be successful.

SPAIN

ESP47
ESP56

Amena

Fact File

Sponsors	Amena, Comunidad Valenciana, Telefonica	**Designers**	Joaquin Coello, Rolf Vrolijk, Javier Panies, Manual Ruiz
Yacht Name	*Bravo España*		
Sail Number	ESP-47, ESP-56 (ex ESP-42)	**Skipper**	Pedro Campos
		Helmsman	Luis Doreste
		Navigator	Joan Vila

Like Japan, Spain is a two-time veteran of the America's Cup having raced in San Diego under the auspices of *España 92* and *Rioja de España 95*. Unlike Japan, neither effort gained a semi-final berth. Underfunded and late to build, both Spanish syndicates arrived on the race course with one-boat campaigns. In 1992, under skipper Pedro Campos, team members had cause to believe they might have caught lightning in a bottle after they won their first two races. But reality soon set in when the stronger teams easily disposed of the rookie effort in round one with margins ranging from 4 to more than 9 minutes at the finish.

Spain struggled through the challengers' second round, winning three races, but accumulating only 14 points to the leader's (New Zealand) 34. Perhaps most telling of the differences between the haves and have-nots was the 13:58 beating the team suffered against eventual Louis Vuitton Cup winner *Il Moro di Venezia*. *España 92* returned home after winning seven of its 21 races and finishing fifth out of eight challengers. The performance was judged creditable enough to try again in 1995.

Rioja de España never had a chance. The boat barely made it out of Spain in time to make it to the starting line in California. The team, once again led by Campos, had only two days of practice before the challenger trials began. They hardly knew their positions and were still testing sails and equipment during the races.

Rioja de España lost its first 15 races. Spain's final numbers were 3-21, but they do not really reflect the consistent improvement shown throughout the challenger trials. The final race against Nippon was close throughout and proved just how far the Spaniards had come. At the finish line, just 13 seconds separated the two boats and Japan won the right to advance into the semi-finals.

In the hope of results being different in Auckland, Spain has once again turned to Pedro Campos who will be joined in the

Pedro Campos (right) has selected Luis Doreste (left) to helm Spain's challenge in Auckland.

cockpit with one of his country's most proven sailors, Luis Doreste.

Although the syndicate has been remarkably quiet, what little is known about Spain's third challenge is all positive. Already more than $US15 million has been raised, chiefly from government sources, the country's royal family and repeat sponsor Telefonica. Like most America's Cup teams of today, a good part of the funds is being spent on design and technology. Spain's entry into the Cup began with the purchase of designs by New Zealander Bruce Farr. Lead designer Joaquin Coello used those plans and the designs and test data from '92 to draw the lines for the '95 racer. But for the Auckland America's Cup, Coello has looked beyond his country's shores for design talent once again.

With many successes in a number of classes, Dutchman Rolf Vrolijk is a significant addition to the Spanish effort. A partner in the German firm of Judel/Vrolijk, the designer is reputed to have free reign in planning the two racing yachts, *ESP-47* and *ESP-56*.

While this edition of the sailing team under the direction of Campos and Doreste might not be mistaken for grizzled veterans, neither should they be considered inexperienced rookies. In 1992 that charge may have had validity, especially given the lack of time on board big boats or on the match-racing circuit, but the situation is different today. Campos and his racing team were frequent match race competitors during the past few years and the two Cup appearances have served the team well. Having reinforced so many areas of the challenge, it is almost unthinkable that Spain will suffer another 0 for 15 start in the 2000 America's Cup.

~ Russell Coutts

The inclusion of Luis Doreste and some of the Olympic sailors immediately means Spain is rated higher than before. It was Luis Doreste

The new Spanish boat *Bravo España* soon after its launch at the CADE base in Valencia's port area.

who beat me in my first world youth championships in 1979 and he has since gone on to win two Olympic gold medals in 1984 and 1992. Spain is one of the most successful nations in terms of Olympic sailing and so it is curious that they have waited this long to use their best talent. The design team are boosted by the inclusion of designer Rolf Vrolijk, who has a highly successful record in IMS racing. The team will come to Auckland after an intensive build-up in Spain using both their old and new boats over several years. This is without question the best Spanish challenge to date.

FRA46

Sixieme
Sens

FRANCE

Fact File

Sponsors	Bouygues Telecom, Transiciel	Designers	Yaka Design Team – Bernard Nivelt, Daniel Andrieu, Philippe Barriere
Yacht Name	*Sixieme Sens*		
Sail Number	FRA-46		
		Helmsman	Bertrand Pacé
		Tactician	Thierry Peponnet
		Navigator	Marcel van Triest

When Le Défi Bouygues Telecom Transiciel syndicate sends its one boat campaign to the starting line in October, France will celebrate its 29th year of America's Cup competition. It was in 1970 that Baron Marcel Bich of the Bic pen and disposable lighter fortune brought his country into the game in rather grand style. While fine wine and remarkable parties were more in evidence than sailing skills (*France* failed to win a race against Australia's *Gretel II*), Bich's white-gloved entry laid a foundation for Cup challenges to come.

In 1974, Bich's same boat lost to Australia again, this time racing the new *Southern Cross*. In 1977, *France* was intended to be merely the trial horse for *France II*, but the new boat proved too slow and the old war-horse was once again commissioned for battle. Finally, mercifully, the yacht was retired after a three-Cup campaign that ended without a victory in 18 races. Bich would have to wait until 1980 to experience his first win when *France 3* was well sailed by skipper Bruno Troublé into the finals against Australia. The Aussies advanced to the America's Cup match against Dennis Conner and *Freedom*, but not before *France* took a race off them.

Bich then announced his retirement from the Cup and sold *France 3* to the film producer Yves Roussert-Rouard. Roussert-Rouard campaigned the yacht in the 1983

challenger trials, the year that Louis Vuitton began sponsoring these races. Troublé, who has since gone on to head the Louis Vuitton efforts associated with the Cup, was once again the helmsman. But his work as marketing director for Bic Marine prevented his full-time on-board presence and coupled with money problems and an inexperienced crew, the challenge was an also-ran.

The Baron Bich era gave way to the Marc Pajot era, which began with great promise but ended badly. A celebrated helmsman in France, Pajot was the logical successor to the America's Cup leadership position. Pajot's initial Cup appearance was in Fremantle, Western Australia, in 1986. Backed by the first corporate single sponsor in Cup history (instant photo concern KIS) and racing a computer-conceived yacht sporting everyone's favourite name – *French Kiss* – Pajot made it into the semi-finals before falling to the Kiwis and their fibreglass speedster.

For the 1992 event in San Diego, Pajot repeated his Fremantle performance by racing his way into the semi-finals, but once again was eliminated during that round. By 1995, the French people had built high expectations for Pajot who arrived in San Diego with a huge budget and a crew of France's sailing elite. But the effort was plagued by severe damage to the yacht that was to be the trial horse and then the loss

Sixieme Sens is one of the more radical looking challenger boats with her extremely narrow beam.

The French crew were reported to be very excited with early performance when the boat was trialled off Laurient.

of that yacht's keel, internecine battles, accusations of mismanagement and, in the end, an ineffectual racing record of 8-16. This time the team did not make it to the semi-finals and more than one French journalist called for Pajot's head.

For the Auckland America's Cup, it became clear early that Pajot was a man without a country. As he looked towards Switzerland, his native land began a youth movement that produced a syndicate called Yaka which initially promised a majority of crew with ages of less than 25. The syndicate looked from the beginning to have the strongest chance of getting Frenchmen to New Zealand. Two other syndicates were formed in the south of France and flirted with establishing ongoing campaigns, but fundraising problems forced a merger into what it now called Le Defi Sud.

Yaka found support from Bouygues Telecom and Transiciel and changed its name to reflect the sponsors. Now known as

Le Défi Bouygues Telecom Transiciel, the syndicate has also made personnel changes, most noticeable in the helmsman position. Bertrand Pacé, France's top-ranked match racer and former (1994) world champion of the discipline, will be at the wheel in Auckland. He has been involved in the past three America's Cup contests, most recently as tactician of the French boat in 1995. Money is tight and syndicate head Luc Gelluseau is banking on advancement to the semi-finals with a one-boat campaign.

The design approach is similar to that of defender Team New Zealand. A team have been formed that includes designers and scientists. They are led by Philippe Paulu de la Barriere whose Cup experience goes back to Baron Bich's *France 3*.

Meanwhile, although Marc Pajot leads his own campaign in Switzerland, he still has something to say about the French effort. Le Defi Sud, strapped for funds, appeared at the time of writing to have only one chance to make it to Auckland. That chance is controlled by Pajot and is in the form of the IACC yacht the Swiss team have used for training. Originally planned for the 1995 Cup, the yacht was only partially finished when acquired by the Swiss. Four months before the Louis Vuitton Cup was scheduled to begin, Le Defi Sud's hope is to raise enough money to charter the yacht. Should that happen, France will have two teams in Auckland, but the reality is that Le Defi Sud would have little chance in a four-year-old boat against the new generation Cup yachts being built around the world. The better chance for a strong showing is Le Défi Bouygues Telecom Transiciel.

~ Russell Coutts

They are marketing themselves as a young team but in reality, they are old campaigners with a lot of experience. Bertrand Pacé and Thierry Peponnet are two of the best big boat sailors France has ever produced. Pacé has been very successful on the match-racing circuit, winning the world championships in 1994. He has built a crew that is among the best in the world. Peponnet steered the tune-up boat for Marc Pajot in 1995. Their design group have adopted a fresh approach and have produced what looks to be a very radical boat. This team have the potential to surprise, yet having only one boat may be a disadvantage.

Thierry Peponnet, an Olympic gold medalist in 1988, will be a key person in the background for 2000.

Luc Gelluseau has run the Corum sailing team since 1990 and is co-manager with Pierre Mas of Le Défi Bouygues Telecom Transiciel.

The design team has created what appears to be a very narrow and radical boat.

France's highest ranked match racer, Bertrand Pacé, has been selected to command the sailing team of Le Défi Bouygues Telecom Transiciel. Pacé won the match racing world championships in 1994.

SUI59

be hAP_{py}

SWITZERLAND

Fact File

Sponsors	Mediterranean	Designers	Phillipe Briand,
	Shipping Company		Peter van Ossannen,
	Computer Ass,		Sebastien Schmidt
	Audemars Piguet	Skipper	Marc Pajot
Yacht Name	*be hAPpy*	Helmsman	Jochen Schumann
Sail Number	SUI-59	Tactician	Enrico Chieffi

As noted earlier, Marc Pajot has crossed the border into a land-locked country perhaps few observers would have considered as an America's Cup hopeful. But Pajot has made the most of this opportunity, forming an international team that feature a German helmsman, an Italian tactician, a French designer, a Dutch/Australian technician, and crew from several European countries. All together, they form the FAST 2000 team.

For more than a year during the lead-up to 1999, it looked as though there would be two teams in Auckland. A second effort, an "all-Swiss" team, was in the making with its nucleus formed from Jean Marc Monard's match-racing team. The young Swiss sailor enjoyed a fast rise on the match race world ranking list, won recognition for his skills and was able to attract some of his country's most talented sailors as well as financial support. But finding sponsorship for the match-racing circuit and for an America's Cup campaign are two entirely different quests. The money wasn't there and the doors closed in 1998, leaving the more experienced Pajot as Switzerland's lone flag carrier into this new venture.

Pajot's choice for helmsman drew immediate attention. Jochen Schumann, winner of three Olympic gold medals, is renowned by his countrymen and respected by the international sailing community. Pajot's decision to give the helm over to Schumann so he can concentrate on the

The Swiss hull during construction being lifted from a female mould.

syndicate leadership role has been viewed as a beneficial move. The employment of Enrico Chieffi as tactician, one of Italy's top sailors who brings Cup experience to the team, also strengthens the effort.

Money problems have slowed progress, but there is considerable optimism within the Swiss camp that a new yacht being constructed will prove to be fast. Heading the design team is Philippe Briand, one of the most experienced Cup designers at work today. He has been teamed with Pajot since the days of *French Kiss*, the semi-finalist in Fremantle. Briand is the author of five IACC racers and the public relations spin on his new creation is that he has hit all the marks.

Much of the design work has been done by computer modelling. Tank testing has been done in England at the same facilities that Team New Zealand use and the Swiss designers and technicians believe it to be more accurate than Briand has used in the past. Before the initial funds ran out, enough modelling and testing were done to allow the team to make a final decision on which design to build. They are confident they have a competitive boat; there are even whispers of a "breakthrough".

Although money has been tight, the emphasis has been on design. The team did spend some time in New Zealand waters, but most of their training has been on Swiss lakes in the French boat planned for San Diego that may be chartered by Esprit-Sud. The new boat has been designed and built specifically for the Hauraki Gulf. The question that remains is will the sailors have enough time on board to tune it, and themselves, properly? It is a question well asked of many of the challengers.

~ Russell Coutts

If their new boat is fast, they could be a contender, but their lack of practice and the fact that they have no tune-up boat will hurt their campaign. Although they have some very good people, they are rated by most as a long shot.

Jochen Schumann, designated helmsman for FAST 2000, has won three Olympic gold medals and is renowned as one of the best sailors in the world.

Philippe Briand, head of FAST 2000's design team, is one of the most experienced Cup designers at work today. He and Marc Pajot have worked together since the days of *French Kiss*.

Marc Pajot made his America's Cup debut in 1986 for France and will be in New Zealand as head of Switzerland's FAST 2000 syndicate.

AUSTRALIA

Fact File

Sponsors	Private funding	**Designers**	Fluid Thinking
Yacht Name	*Sydney 95*	**Skipper**	Syd Fischer
Sail Number	AUS-29	**Helmsman**	James Spithill

An America's Cup event, particularly in the Southern Hemisphere, without an entry from Australia is unthinkable. Since 1962, when *Gretel* took a race off *Weatherly*, the Aussies have been major players in the Cup game.

Although the country suffered through winless contests with *Dame Pattie* (1967), *Southern Cross* (1974) and *Australia* (1977), a strong foundation was being built. *Gretel*'s race win in the America's Cup match was followed by one in 1970 (*Gretel II*) and another in 1980 (*Australia*). While this may not seem too impressive, consider that as a challenger, the Australian yachts beat back all their competition to advance to the Cup match. The hurdle remained the Americans with their unequalled depth of experience, talent and resources.

That hurdle was overcome in 1983 by Alan Bond's money, Ben Lexcen's wing keel, Warren Jones' political savvy, and John Bertrand's sailing and leadership talent. The great victory that brought the end to America's 132-year winning streak pumped new life into the Cup and made the event a truly international competition.

The racing that took place in the wild and woolly Indian Ocean was an unqualified success, viewed by many as the best America's Cup in history. Australia played the perfect host, extending its gracious hospitality to all visitors by not only offering what may have been the perfect venue, but by playing the friendly villain in Dennis Conner's emotional comeback scenario. For America's Cup aficionados, it was the best of times.

There is a theory that had Australia not won the trophy in 1983, many of the challengers who have since entered the game may not have done so without the proof that America could be beaten. After all, it had been 132 years and before 1983 the matches had never really been even close. Since that time, Japan, Spain, Switzerland and New Zealand have mounted actual campaigns while Russia, Hong Kong, Germany, and the US Virgin Islands have formed syndicates later disbanded because of lack of funds.

Add to the country's history the most extraordinary event in America's Cup history. The dramatic sinking of *oneAustralia* while racing in 1995 off the coast of California generated not only worldwide front-page headlines, but also the realisation of a needed balance between design and engineering innovation and just plain safety. No doubt the *oneAustralia* experience played a part in the thinking of every designer, technician, engineer, and builder who are sending boats to Auckland.

Australia is poised to make history once again in the person of Syd Fischer, the fifth attempt by the man called "Nails", a record equal to that of Sir Thomas Lipton. His Young Australia 2000 also features the youngest skipper ever to helm an America's Cup entry – Sydney native James Spithill, aged 19. True to the syndicate's name, and comparable to the approach of France's le défi Bouygues Telecom Transiciel, the crew will consist of 11 sailors aged 18-22 and

four experienced "mentor sailors". The young sailors are being selected from various youth programmes at Australia's leading yacht clubs.

Fischer's attempts in 1983 (*Advance*) and 1992 (*Challenge Australia*) are perhaps better left forgotten as they were well off the pace. But his 1987 (*Sydney Steak 'n' Kidney*) and 1995 (*Sydney*) had the makings of real contenders. In fact, there are those within the Cup community who still believe *Steak 'n' Kidney* had the potential to be the fastest boat in Fremantle had it been allowed to fully develop during the Royal Perth Yacht Club's defence selection series.

This time Fischer is the only challenger from his country and he is beholden to no one. Fischer is well known in sailing circles as his own man, an individual who not only marches to his own drum but pays no heed to the beat. As an official challenger who paid the quarter-million-dollar bill to join the party, he has the right to make his opinions known on Cup issues. And he has.

When the prices for syndicate compound space in Auckland were originally announced, Fischer led the protest over what was seen as exorbitant rates. Although they have been reduced and the real estate has been leased, Fischer maintains he and his challenge will operate from their own barge moored in the harbour just off the pricey Cup village.

Fischer also led the dissent over some unnamed syndicates' second thoughts about the semi-final format after challengers had voted to allow six boats into the competition. He also insisted upon clarification of money distribution from television and other licensing rights. It is fair to say that he has not gone quietly into his fifth campaign, but then again, who more than Fischer has earned the right to question the rules?

This is not a man who is accustomed to either losing or being told what to do. In sport he has competed in and won almost all of the most prestigious ocean races including the Admiral's Cup, the One Ton Cup, the Kenwood Cup, the Fastnet Race, and, perhaps most important to him, the Sydney to Hobart Race. Few, if any, have had the better of him.

Also involved in Young Australia 2000 is Sir James Hardy, whose Cup experience goes all the way back to when he drove

Gretel II in the 1970 match. Hardy is revered in the Australian sailing community and his soft-spoken manner seems the perfect foil to Fischer's more excitable demeanour.

No doubt by the time the team cross the Tasman to compete in Auckland, attention will be on Spithill, on the young sailors, on the racing yacht, and on the team's chances for advancement. But there is no question that the spotlight will still shine on Syd Fischer.

~ Russell Coutts

Syd Fischer is back again but this time is using his old boat from 1995. Even if it is modified, it is hard to imagine it will be competitive against the 1999 generation.

Fischer has hired a very young crew and is presumably looking to develop experience for future America's Cups.

Stars & Stripes met *Kookaburra III* in the 1987 Cup off the coast of Western Australia. The US boat prevailed, sending the event to California.

Few men in Australian sailing circles can match the record of Sir James Hardy, whose Cup experience goes all the way back to when he drove *Gretel II* in the 1970 match. He has helped organise the Young Australia 2000 team.

Iain Murray has been a key part of Australia's America's Cup history since 1987 as both a designer and skipper.

With Alan Bond's backing, *Australia II* turned the America's Cup world upside down with the greatest upset in the event's then 132-year history when the yacht beat Dennis Conner's *Liberty* in 1983.

Syd Fischer is a legendary figure in international sailing competitions and will tie Sir Thomas Lipton's record of backing five America's Cup challengers when his Young Australia 2000 heads to the New Zealand starting line.

Ben Lexcen, chief designer of *Australia II*, holds the trophy his boat won in Australia's seventh America's Cup challenge.

Australia II's skipper John Bertrand prompts a laugh from Eileen Bond during the magical fall, for Australians, of 1983.

ALOHA RACING

USA50
USA54

Abracadabra
2000

Fact File

Sponsors	Healthsouth, Columbia Sportswear Co, P&O Nedlloyd	Designers	Andy Dovell, Ian Burns
		Helmsman	John Kolius
Yacht Name	*Abracadabra*		
Sail Number	USA-50, USA-54		

"Abracadabra" is defined by *Webster's Dictionary* as "a magical word once held to avert disease or disaster". Dr Jim Andrews, chairman of the Aloha Racing challenge for the America's Cup, has used the word to name his string of ocean racing yachts over the past decade and their successes have averted disaster to date. The good doctor must have uttered the word more than once when it appeared the disease of insufficient funds common to many Cup syndicates, might be terminal. But an infusion of dollars from the company HealthSouth was enough to complete the design and construction programmes that will produce two IACC racers (sail numbers USA-50 and USA-54) and get the team from Hawaii to New Zealand.

If Andrews is a novice at the game, his chosen skipper, John Kolius, is a veteran. Often acting as helmsman on the *Abracadabra*s, Kolius has worked well with Andrews since 1990. His skills at the wheel of a sailboat first received international recognition in 1983 when Kolius and the 10-year-old *Courageous* advanced to the finals of the defence trials where they met Conner and *Liberty*. The new kid on the block with the old boat outdid expectations, but Conner and his new boat performed better and received the tip of the straw hat from the club's selection committee.

The way Kolius had handled both his boat and himself impressed the New Yorkers. After Conner and *Liberty* lost to *Australia II* and its wing keel, the club turned to Kolius to lead the way to Fremantle.

But, unwittingly, Kolius found himself in the centre of a controversy. When he was asked to sign an agreement that stated he wouldn't build sails for his own campaign, he refused. This, added to internal political strife and syndicate management problems, brought to the surface a number of brewing conflicts and Kolius saw no alternative but to resign.

Now with its house in disarray, the club received an ultimatum from two men who had loaned it $US3million to organise the Cup campaign: give us the money back or step aside and we'll call the shots. When

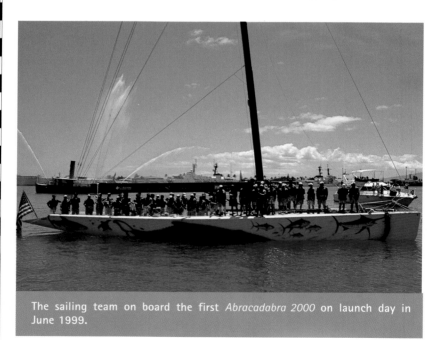

The sailing team on board the first *Abracadabra 2000* on launch day in June 1999.

club members came to understand they had lost control of their own syndicate, they agreed to a reorganisation. Kolius returned, but what had once been the stronghold of Cup defence had displayed its weakness as a challenger and the campaign arrived in Australia somewhat stunned and wounded.

Its failure to advance to even the semi-finals (losing out to *French Kiss* by one point) proved unbearable for many of the club's members and was a contributing factor to the more-than-10-year hiatus from Cup competition.

While the New York Yacht Club stepped to the sidelines, Kolius stayed involved in Cup campaigns as coach of the Il Moro di Venezia team in 1992 and the America[3] women's team in 1995. But the desire to fulfil the promise he exhibited in 1983 pushed him to return as skipper and helmsman.

Under the official auspices of the Waikiki Yacht Club, Aloha Racing was established to "bring the America's Cup to Paradise". It seems an ideal set-up for Kolius. He has complete control of the sailing operations; but perhaps most important, the team believe the wind and wave conditions are very similar to those in Auckland. Unlike many of the other challengers, Aloha Racing did not train in New Zealand before the Louis Vuitton Cup, but this may not be a disadvantage if their home base proves their theory.

Designers Andy Dovell and Ian Burns, veterans of the design teams that produced *oneAustralia* in 1995 and *Spirit of Australia* in 1992, have gone the computer-modelling and tank-testing route in the absence of a syndicate-owned IACC boat. The team's first boat was launched in early June 1999 as the second yacht *Abracadara 2000* (sail number USA-50, with USA-54 assigned to the second boat) was completing construction, further proof Kolius aims to avert the disaster that befell him the last time he ventured Down Under.

~ Russell Coutts

John Kolius is an experienced campaigner. He has assembled two new boats which the crew have been shaking down in Hawaii. Their design team draw upon much of the talent from oneAustralia*'s 1995 effort, so their boats should be competitive. They have some excellent crew who should be able to optimise their boats.*

The construction crew of *Abracadabra 2000* poses in front of a mural painted for the team by the renowned marine artist Wyland. His work is also prominently displayed on the hull of the racing boats.

John Kolius first appeared in America's Cup competition in 1986 in Australia as the skipper of the New York Yacht Club's first effort as a challenger. He'll race in New Zealand as skipper of the Aloha Racing challenge from Hawaii.

Dr Jim Andrews is one of America's leading orthopaedic surgeons and an avid sailor. His contributions to the Hawaiian syndicate have been immeasurable.

AMERICAONE

USA49
USA61

AmericaOne

Fact File

Sponsors	Ford-Visteon, Telcordia/SAIC, Hewlett Packard, United Technologies	Yacht Name	*AmericaOne*
		Sail Number	USA-49, USA-61
		Designer	Bruce Nelson
		Helmsman	Paul Cayard
		Tactician	John Kostecki
		Navigator	Terry Hutchinson

Things looked pretty good when in early 1996 the venerable St Francis Yacht Club, hard on the shores of San Francisco Bay, announced that it was giving official sanction to an America's Cup syndicate named AmericaOne, led by favourite son Paul Cayard. Cayard, a veteran of three America's Cup campaigns and a perennial star on the match-racing circuit, introduced James H. Clark as AmericaOne's chairman, a position he also held at Netscape Communications, the Internet browser company he had co-founded.

Joining the group were designer Bruce Nelson, who traced his Cup origins to Dennis Conner's design team that produced the victorious boat coming out of Fremantle. He also worked with Conner on his 1988 catamaran defence and helped design the *Young America* yacht Cayard had steered in the '95 Cup. Laurent Esquier came on board as operations director. He worked with Conner in '83, is credited with teaching the crew of the first New Zealand challenge how to handle 12-metre yachts in '86/'87 and was with *Il Moro* in 1992.

As the team began to form, they presented a strong profile. Fundraising prospects appeared solid, drawing on the wealthy yacht club membership, the San Francisco corporate community and nearby Silicon Valley. But within six months, things turned sour. Clark resigned to devote more time to Netscape.

Esquier left when Italy's Prada made him an offer he couldn't refuse. Several marketing managers came and went. Another Cup syndicate, America True, set up shop just across the bay, undercutting AmericaOne's solo position in the San Francisco area. Money dried up and rumours of the effort ending spread along international docks.

After several tense weeks of meetings and strategy sessions, the ship was righted. St Francis member George "Fritz" Jewett Jr took over as vice-chairman of the Board of Directors and some semblance of order was restored. Jewett brought some 25 years of America's Cup experience to the position. In 1974 he served as co-chairman of the Intrepid syndicate, then chairman of Enterprise in 1977. From 1980 to 1995 he supported Dennis Conner in a number of capacities and Conner credits him with getting him back into Cup competition after 1983's loss to Australia when the skipper contemplated quitting the Cup for good. Jewett is one of the most savvy Cup individuals in the world.

Yet just as some of the holes in the leaking syndicate were being plugged, Cayard announced he would skipper *EF Language* in the Whitbread Round the World Race. It was a tremendously risky move, leaving a fledgling Cup campaign at a vulnerable time. But the gamble paid off when Cayard became the first American to win the gruelling contest, collecting valuable media coverage for more than a year. During stopovers, Cayard flew home to bolster fundraising activities.

In less than 90 days from the conclusion of the Whitbread, AmericaOne closed on two significant sponsorships: Telcordia Technologies/SAIC and Ford Motor Company. Add to those the Hewlett-Packard Company United Technologies and it's clear that AmericaOne will be a force to be reckoned with in New Zealand.

Yet true to the seesaw nature of the campaign, bad news has been mixed with the good. Steve Erickson, one of Cayard's closest friends and long-time crewman, was coaxed away by Prada to help coach. Kimo Worthington, a Bay area resident and member of the America[3] team in both '92

and '95, defected to arch-rival Young America. Cayard was stung by the two exits, but when rumours began to swirl that John Kostecki was being wooed by Young America, he fought hard to keep the tactician in the AmericaOne fold.

Kostecki won the Olympic silver medal in the Soling Class in 1988 and has been among sailing's elite ever since. In 1997 he won the Mumm 36 World Championship, the One Design 48 Championship and the Malaysia Challenge Grand Prix. He also sailed in the Whitbread aboard *Chessie Racing* as co-helmsman/tactician and is credited with improving the boat's performance significantly. Kostecki is joined on the AmericaOne sailing team by a

AmericaOne is reported to be very narrow. This photo shows her very flat topsides and extended corners aft in an attempt to gain additional sailing length when the yacht is heeled.

number of other world-class sailors including Terry Hutchinson, Josh Belsky, Curtis Blewett, and Sean Clarkson.

Nelson has remained on board as the principal designer. His experience is a key component of AmericaOne's hopes. Before joining Conner's design team for the Fremantle Cup, he won recognition for several successful ocean-racing yachts. His work on *Stars & Stripes* was his first ever on a 12-metre and likewise on the 60ft catamaran in 1988. In 1992 he was involved in the Partnership for America's Cup Technology (PACT) which was established as a reservoir of scientific and technological knowledge and resources from which the defence syndicates could draw. PACT developed into PACT '95 and Nelson served as the lead designer on *Young America*.

As the architect of the boat that lost to New Zealand 5-0, Nelson knows better than most what the challengers are up against. The Kiwis have a huge head start on everyone attempting to win the trophy, but Nelson perhaps has the best idea of exactly what that head start entails. No doubt considerable time has been spent comparing his design to that of the black boats.

Considering that Cayard has been behind the wheel in both the '92 and '95 America's Cup matches, the only two contests that have used IACC yachts, it is fair to say he comes to Auckland with more experience than all the other challengers. How much of an edge that will give him and his team will be answered on the Hauraki Gulf.

~ Russell Coutts
Not only is Paul Cayard one of the favourites among the media, but he is also quick to

Paul Cayard (right, pictured here with Team New Zealand's Sir Peter Blake) hopes to reach the Cup match for the third consecutive time and add the trophy to his Whitbread victory.

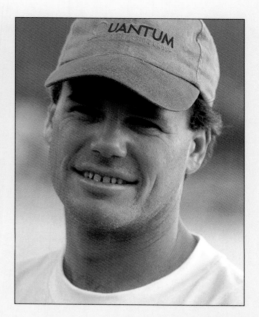

Terry Hutchinson is one of many world-class sailors recruited for the AmericaOne effort.

Above: AmericaOne's training yacht, formerly *oneAustralia*, is pictured outside the team's New Zealand compound.

Right: Designer Bruce Nelson (white hat) shares the afterguard with Paul Cayard as the two teams from San Francisco spar with each other in New Zealand during February 1999.

promote that image himself! The AmericaOne public relations programme seems to be one of the most prominent among the challengers. This has led many people to rate them as the favourites to win the Louis Vuitton Cup. They have a strong sailing team with a very credible record and Cayard has lots of Cup experience. John Kostecki has a lower profile than Cayard, but is a fantastic sailor and it will be an advantage to have him as tactician.

Bruce Nelson was hired as AmericaOne's principal designer. Nelson was co-designer for Dennis Conner's victorious Stars & Stripes challenge in 1987. He was retained as Conner's designer in 1992 and worked for Young America in 1995, bringing with him a lot of Cup design experience.

The team spent several months sailing the revamped OneAustralia in Auckland conditions over the New Zealand summer of 1998-1999 and the syndicate launched and tested the first new boat in Long Beach. They will be strong contenders.

AMERICA TRUE

Fact File

Sponsors	Private funding, Itronix	**Designers**	Phil Kaiko, Heiner Meldner
Yacht Name	*America True*	**Helmsman**	John Cutler
Sail Number	USA-51	**Tactician**	Leslie Egnot

Dawn Riley is arguably the best known woman sailor in America. Adding to her portfolio of two Whitbread Round the World Races and positions on two America's Cup teams, she is now the first woman to manage a Cup team. As CEO and captain of *America True*, affiliated with the San Francisco Yacht club, Riley has put together a co-ed team that is a mixture of sailors with and without Cup experience. Her credo has been to select the best person for the job, regardless of sex, race or religion.

While the focus of America True has certainly been on preparing for the races in Auckland, the syndicate has also designed a programme that uses sailing to teach at-risk youth the fundamentals of team building and operating a sailboat. It is a noble goal that has been applauded and one that well illustrates the full potential of the sport.

In the early days of America True, it was questionable just how successful Riley and her philosophies would be. Altruism is one thing, but finding the millions of dollars needed to fund a campaign is another. Luckily for Riley, G. Christopher Coffin shared her vision and in early 1997 came on board as a significant contributor and assumed the position of chief operating officer. According to America True: "The combination of Mr Coffin's entrepreneurial experience, interest in technology, and passion for sailing have made bringing back the Cup an all-consuming project for Mr Coffin and his family."

According to syndicate members and outside observers, his business and financial savvy is the major reason for America True's success in the fundraising arena and its assurance of a place on the starting line in Auckland.

Making good on her promise of a co-ed team, Riley has recruited experienced Cup campaigners from the 1995 America[3] women's team. Leslie Egnot has signed on as tactician. Behind the wheel in the last Cup, she brings a wealth of sailing experience as well as a knowledge of New Zealand waters, having lived there since 1972. She is joined by fellow Cubers Merritt Carey on the foredeck and trimmer Katie Pettibone. Liz Baylis, an experienced big-boat sailor, will perform cockpit duties.

New Zealander John Cutler will steer. A 1988 Olympic bronze medallist in the demanding Finn Class, he was tactician and then helmsman for the Nippon challenge in 1992 and 1995. He is a veteran of the international match-racing circuit, competing at a top level during the past decade.

Ben Beer, a resident of St Thomas in the U.S. Virgin Islands, is also frequent crew on match races and will begin racing with America True after he competes in the Pan American Games in Finns. He'll work the foredeck at the America's Cup.

What may prove to be America True's greatest asset is more than five years of technical research reportedly worth $US60 million, developed by the America[3] syndicate. The research helped create two fast racing yachts, 1992 Cup winner

America³ and *Mighty Mary* in 1995. One of the design team members who worked on that project was Phil Kaiko, who also worked in the oneAustralia programme in '95 and is now the chief designer for America True.

And another asset from *America³* is Buddy Melges, America's dean of sailors. Only he and Kiwi Russell Coutts can claim ownership of an Olympic gold medal and an America's Cup victory. A few of his other sailing accomplishments include two Star World Championships; a Pan Am Games gold medal in the Flying Dutchman; five E-Scow and seven Skeeter ice boat national championships. He has been selected as the Rolex Yachtsman of the Year three times.

Riley is a proven winner and has amply demonstrated her leadership abilities. Like all challengers, the success of America True will probably be determined by just how fast a boat is designed and built.

America True on the water with CEO Dawn Riley (pictured in foreground) working the line, helmsman John Cutler at the wheel and tactician Leslie Egnot next to him.

~ Russell Coutts

America True were the first team to arrive in Auckland with their new boat and a trial boat, having purchased Chris Dickson's 1995 boat Tag Heuer. *They sailed* Tag *against* oneAustralia *and developed a new mast during the New Zealand summer of 1998-99.*

Sail designer Mike Schreiber will definitely add strength to their sail programme and David Barnes will add a lot of experience to their test programme.

They are not highly rated in sailing circles internationally, but this team could develop the boat speed required, and could surprise.

Leslie Egnot made her America's Cup debut in 1995 on the America[3] women's team. She'll serve in America True's afterguard.

New Zealander John Cutler is the designated helmsman and the head of sailing operations for the co-ed team.

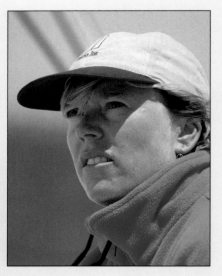

America True's Dawn Riley is the first female CEO of an America's Cup team in the event's long history.

The famous Golden Gate Bridge is depicted on America True's training yacht.

Left: Buddy Melges is the only American to have won an Olympic gold medal and an America's Cup title. He is America True's sailing coach.
Right: Although Bill Koch will sit out this Cup after winning in 1992 and backing the women's team in 1995, his presence is felt in America True, beneficiaries of some $US60 million dollars of his research and technology.

The team spent several months training on the America's Cup course in New Zealand. Here crew member Katie Pettibone trims a sail off Rangitoto Island.

America True seen sailing in early June '99 trials on the Waitemata Harbour.

TEAM DENNIS CONNER

USA55

Stars & Stripes

Fact File

Sponsors	Citizen Watches	Designers	Reichel/Pugh
Yacht Name	*Stars & Stripes*	Skipper	Dennis Conner
Sail Number	USA-55	Helmsman	Ken Read
		Tactician	Peter Holmberg

No one will be seen on the America's Cup course beginning in October 1999 with more experience in the game than Dennis Conner. It is arguable that no other individual has had a greater impact on the America's Cup than "D.C." When he takes his team to the starting line in Auckland for the 1999/2000 competition, he will be sailing in his eighth America's Cup. He is the only man ever to have won the trophy four times and lost it twice.

Conner is often said to have single-handedly changed Cup preparations from a summer vocation to a full-time "ocCupation". It is a charge he denies, but there is no question that he was instrumental in establishing the long campaign in which crew and sail training stretched from a few months to a period of more than a year. Conner was also in the forefront of the move from amateur status to commercial sponsorship. Other skippers and syndicate heads may have come to the party with a great deal more money, but few have been better at garnering financial support in corporate boardrooms and the living rooms of the wealthy than Dennis Conner.

Like most individuals who have achieved the pinnacle of their chosen endeavour, Conner has been involved in more than a few controversies and has collected his detractors through the years. But it is rare to hear anything but praise and almost reverence from anyone who has ever campaigned with him. "My guys" as Conner calls his crew, often refer to their skipper's motivational skills when explaining their deep loyalty to him.

There are innumerable stories of Conner as a boy, walking the docks of the San Diego Yacht Club, asking anyone with a mast on his boat if he needed crew. He had decided at a young age to learn everything he could about the sport and he dedicated himself to that education. He became so familiar to the members of the club that he was offered a junior membership – the youngest person ever to join.

Conner's name first drew attention from the sailing world as a Star sailor. This almost 23-foot boat epitomises real sailing to Conner. To this day, he believes his five victories in the 1977 Star Worlds (he also won in 1971) are his greatest accomplishments in the sport. He also believes Star sailors are a hitch above all others on sailing's food chain.

Over the years, Conner has collected a room full of trophies including an Olympic bronze medal in the Tempest Class, but it is his America's Cup racing that has made him a legend. First invited by Ted Turner to join him in the cockpit of *Mariner* for the defender trials of 1974, Conner quickly exhibited his skills and was promoted to starting helmsman aboard *Courageous*, the eventual Cup victor. In 1980 he skippered *Freedom* to victory, lost aboard *Liberty* in

'83, won in Fremantle three years later, countered Michael Fay's "Big Boat" with a catamaran in '88, lost in the defender trials to Bill Koch's *America³* in '92, and lost the Cup match in '95 to the Kiwis.

For more than a quarter-century, Conner has been at the forefront of sailing's most prestigious regatta and one would think everything there is to be known about the man is on public display. But just the opposite is true. A 1987 *Time* magazine profile of Conner perhaps put it best: "No more enigmatic character presides over any sport. At the top of his game, Conner can eat with Nicklaus, drink with Namath, offend with McEnroe, spend with Marcos and lose with Napoleon."

And for the New Zealand event, Team

Dennis Conner is perhaps the greatest enigma of all the challengers. About all that was known about this group until just a few months before the Louis Vuitton Cup was scheduled to begin was that Dennis was among the official challengers. While most of his would-be opponents were flooding media fax machines and e-mail addresses with details of their progress in fundraising, design, team building, and crew training, Conner sat silent. As usual, rumours stalked him: he has no money; he is fully funded; he has no designers; he has a secret design

Perhaps the most famous match in America's Cup history, Conner drives *Liberty* against *Australia II* in 1983.

team; he isn't going to Auckland; he's moved to Auckland permanently.

In the spring of '99, Conner's long-time lieutenant Bill Trenkle finally set the record straight – sort of. It was announced that Peter Holmberg, America's top-ranked match racer and former head of the dying Virgin Islands challenge, was joining Conner. Then came word that Ken Read, one of America's bright young sailors with '95 Cup experience, was selected as helmsman. He and Holmberg then hit the match-race circuit and, with the Virgin Islander at the wheel, they won the Congressional Cup.

Contrary to his lengthy training programmes of the past, Conner's philosophy now appears to be something along the line of "We all know how to race a sailboat, just give me a good boat". He's relying on the design talents of John Reichel and Jim Pugh to do just that. The two were part of the design teams of both *America³* and *oneAustralia* and have designed a number of trophy winners.

While some of the questions surrounding Conner's eighth run at the Cup have been answered, many remain. Will the man who invented the two-boat campaign be handicapped by building just one boat (sail number USA-55, the same number that adorned his *Stars & Stripes* in his Fremantle comeback victory)?

Conner will be 56 years old during the challenger trials and some wonder if his more relaxed approach to Cup preparations may be a concession to age. Detractors point to the calendar to explain his 19th place in the 1998 Etchells Worlds, a regatta he has formerly done well in. Supporters point out when he was at the helm of *Toshiba* in the Whitbread, he finished the leg in second place. They will also remind a listener that Buddy Melges steered *America³* to victory in 1992 at the age of 62. But one wonders if Conner's decision to hire two hot-shot helmsmen in Holmberg and Read is a signal he won't be behind the wheel in Auckland.

Somehow that seems an impossibility, as hard to believe as any modern America's Cup without a Team Dennis Conner.

~ Russell Coutts

Conner is probably the most famous sailor in the world, but it was 1988 when he last won the America's Cup. He has assembled a strong afterguard with Ken Read, Peter Holmberg and Peter Isler. Isler was navigator for Conner in Fremantle and with Holmberg and Read will form one of the strongest afterguards among the challengers.

The designers are Reichel and Pugh, who were heavily involved in the oneAustralia programme for 1995.

They have built only one new boat and started their sailing preparations late, launching in September. This may prove to be a big disadvantage against some of the other well-prepared syndicates. For this reason, I find it difficult to rate their chances of winning the Louis Vuitton Cup, but Conner has surprised many people many times.

Dennis Conner's *Stars & Stripes* arriving in Tauranga, New Zealand, ready for a September launch.

He's been called "Mr America's Cup" and for good reason. Dennis Conner will be making his eighth appearance in the event when he and his team travel to New Zealand.

Below: Peter Holmberg was the co-founder of the Virgin Islands America's Cup Challenge before merging with Team Dennis Conner. He'll be in the afterguard during racing in Auckland.

Above: The new *Stars & Stripes* under sail in Auckland.

Above: Bill Trenkle has raced with Conner for years and heads to Auckland as operations manager for the American challenger.

Right: Two of a long list of loyal sailors Conner calls "my guys", Peter Isler and Tom Whidden helped the skipper win in Fremantle.

USA53
USA58

Young
America

YOUNG AMERICA

Fact File

Sponsors	Air New Zealand, Helly-Hansen, Brown & Sharpe, Mullen Advertising, Wihelmsen Lines, Yale Cordage, *Yachting* Magazine, Private funding	Yacht Name	*Young America*
		Sail Number	USA-53, USA-58
		Designers	Bruce Farr, Duncan MacLane
		Helmsman	Ed Baird
		Tactician	Tony Rey
		Navigator	Ed Adams
		Others	Jim Brady, Kimo Worthington

On paper, the New York Yacht Club's Young America syndicate looks like the overwhelming favourite of the challengers. At the head of the effort is John Marshall, who dates his Cup involvement back to 1974 with *Intrepid*. He serves as president and chief executive officer of the Young America challenge.

Marshall graduated from Harvard College with a degree in biochemistry and has also studied at the Rockefeller Institute and Stevens Institute of Technology. His scientific background served him well as manager of the *Stars & Stripes* design teams in the 1987 and 1988 Cup events. His sailing background includes winning an Olympic bronze medal in 1972 in the Dragon Class and as mainsail trimmer aboard *Freedom* ('80) and *Liberty* ('83). These dual disciplines give him a solid foundation as the man most responsible for organising Young America.

On the design side, Marshall hired two of the most experienced and recognised names in the sailing world. Duncan MacLane is the syndicate's design/technology manager. His experience in the Cup arena includes co-designer of *Heart of America* in 1987 and design team leader of the *Stars & Stripes* catamaran in 1988.

The syndicate refers to Farr Yacht Design

Ltd as its "principal designer". President and founder of the concern, Bruce Farr may be the most sought-after racing sailboat designer in the world. Farr was on the design teams that created New Zealand's first America's Cup entry in 1987, Michael Fay's "Big Boat" in 1988, New Zealand's challenge in 1992, and Chris Dickson's *Tag Heuer* in 1995. Failure to win the Cup is the one outstanding blemish on an otherwise stellar career and there is little doubt his work for Young America is receiving his most intense attention.

Skipper Ed Baird leads the sailing team. Baird's name received international recognition in 1995 as sailing coach of Cup winner Team New Zealand, as skipper of the victorious team that won the World Championship of Match-Race Sailing, as being ranked number one on the match-race ranking, and as the recipient of the Rolex Yachtsman of the Year award. For Young America he oversees crew recruitment and he has helped organise an on-water team that boasts 17 Cup victories among the individual members. Among them are: Stu Argo, Tom Burnham, Steve Calder, Bill Cambell, Jamie Gale and Ross Halcrow (both members of Team New Zealand in 1995), Hartwell Jordan, Tony Rey, Grant Spanhake, and Kimo Worthington. Baird has also been an integral part of the research and development phase of the syndicate's agenda by managing the sailing side of the two-boat testing programme.

Young America have used two of the better 1995 International America's Cup Class yachts as their training platforms. *Young America*, the race boat used by the PACT '95 group and later sailed by Team Dennis Conner in the Cup match, was part of the assets turned over to the new syndicate. The acquisition of the Farr-designed *Tag Heuer* provided the second boat on which sail, gear and crew training has taken place on the waters off Rhode Island in 1997 and 1998.

Complementing Young America's on-the-water testing is the syndicate's reliance on computer modelling, tank testing and wind tunnel work. Like almost all Cup contenders operating today, the syndicate also uses velocity prediction programs (VPPs), one of the most important tools designers use. VPPs give designers the ability to estimate the maximum potential speed of a sailboat in a given wind condition which allows them to compare two or more designs.

Dr Jerry Milgram, a professor at the Massachusetts Institute of Technology and one of Bill Koch's designers in 1992 and 1995, is a true believer in VPPs. He has brought that belief to Young America for this America's Cup, as well as the use of the sailing dynamometer, a model that measures sail forces directly on a sailboat. Computers record outputs from sailing instruments which provide wind speed and direction, boat speed, heel angle, heading, etc. When this

data is compared against that from other designs, the result is the most accurate VPPs modern technology can achieve.

How well Milgram, Marshall, MacLane, Farr and the rest of the design team interpret that data and translate it to the builders at Goetz Custom Boats, who have built more America's Cup boats than anyone else in the world, may just determine where the trophy resides after March 2000.

Young America being put through early trials soon after arriving in Auckland.

Floridian Ed Baird is the designated helmsman for the New York Yacht Club's Young America Challenge.

John Marshall brings more than 20 years of America's Cup experience to his position as president and CEO of Young America.

Jim Brady was Team Dennis Conner's navigator in the 1995 Cup and will sail with Young America in New Zealand.

Kimo Worthington was part of the victorious America[3] team in 1992 and director of sailing operations for the women's team in 1995. He works closely with skipper Ed Baird and the Young America sailing team.

The Young America team that trained in Auckland at the end of 1998 poses for a portrait aboard the yacht that competed in the '95 Cup match against Team New Zealand.

Eric Goetz is building both *Young America* yachts for the Auckland battles. He has built more IACC boats than anyone in the world.

Bruce Farr is considered one of the world's foremost racing yacht designers. His America's Cup boats have been involved in every event since New Zealand's famous fibreglass 12-metres in 1986. His talents are in the employ of Young America for America's Cup 2000.

Boatspeed is one thing, but how it is harnessed during battle transfers the game from designers to sailors. Baird and his all-world crew know this as well as any of the challengers and they have covered more than 3000 miles in practice on Rhode Island Sound. They have also trained on the America's Cup course in Auckland.

On paper, this team looks to be an overwhelming favourite, but it might be well served to remember history. The New York Yacht Club's America II syndicate seemed made of the same ingredients in 1986 before they disintegrated in the waters Down Under. Have important lessons been learned and will the America's Cup be returned to the yacht club that founded the trophy? Stay tuned.

~ Russell Coutts

Many have downgraded Young America's chances because of their sailing team's less than stellar performances over the past few seasons. However, the America's Cup in many ways is a technology race and Young America have a team capable of producing a fast boat.

Bruce Farr is reported to have had use of the lion's share of the resources, but he is yet to design a winning America's Cup boat. They have used extensive tank testing and scientific resources to design their boats. There is every reason to expect that this may become Farr's best design effort yet.

The sailing team have had two summers testing in Newport, Rhode Island, and skipper Ed Baird has won the match-racing worlds before, in 1995. They have some extremely capable sailors who have proven that they can win but they will need to be at their peak. Their new boats were launched very late, possibly for security reasons, which may ultimately prove to be an advantage or disadvantage! It seems it is a syndicate that has the potential to win the Louis Vuitton Cup.

AGE OF RUSSIA

~ Russell Coutts

If the Russians make it to the starting line, it will be a miracle, but fantastic. They are using an old boat, built for 1992 but never sailed. Although they will not be a serious challenge, it would be great to have a Russian team in the event. The Russians have a very creditable Olympic sailing history with many great sailors and Olympic medalists. They have very little big boat experience but could technically, as a nation, be able to mount a serious challenge if they chose to, drawing on their small boat champions. For this Cup however, don't expect them to be competitive.

CHAPTER 7

Racing One on One

Tactically, the modern America's Cup is different from most sailing regattas which are fleet races where a number of boats compete against each other. This was actually the format of the 100 Guinea Cup which led to the establishment of the America's Cup as the yacht *America* took on 15 British vessels. The word "match" in the original Deed of Gift has led to a number of disagreements over its exact definition, but it has come to define the format of the modern America's Cup. In fact, match racing, in which one boat races another, has been the style of competition in this regatta since 1871.

For spectators, match racing is easy to understand because it's simple to determine which of the two boats is leading. For helmsmen and crew, match racing demands excellent team work and quick reactions. Position on the course relative to the other boat is key. It is not necessary to sail around the course as fast as possible. Often sailing extra distances in order to control a position or force the opponent further behind is more beneficial. The strategy for match racing has been loosely described as "trying to figure out where the opponent wants to be and then getting in the way!"

Because the America's Cup is not a regularly scheduled event, the match-racing format, with its unique strategies and tactics, was not universally practised until the early 1980s. At that time, a circuit of match-racing events began to develop worldwide, allowing skippers, crews and umpires to refine and test their skills. Today, more than 1200 international teams are ranked and hundreds of match-race regattas are held each year. The sport is constantly changing as crews continually experiment and adopt new techniques in an effort to outsmart their opponents. Most of the skippers and crews who will compete in the 1999/2000 America's Cup races have been competitors on the match-racing circuit.

When the Challenger Trials begin in Auckland in October 1999, each of the challengers will compete in four round robins that will lead to a semi-final series and then to a final match of two challenger yachts. The winner will then face Team New Zealand in the America's Cup match. That match will consist of up to nine races, the winner being the first yacht to record five wins.

Let's now consider some of the key tactics and strategies that spectators and television viewers will observe during the racing.

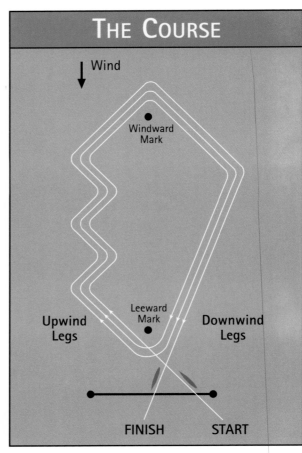

THE COURSE

Wind

Windward Mark

Upwind Legs

Leeward Mark

Downwind Legs

FINISH   START

THE TWO BASIC RULES OF SAILING

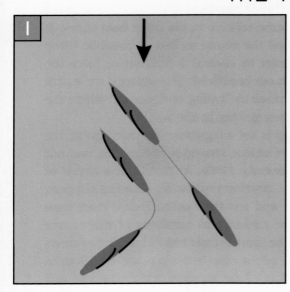

1. PORT AND STARBOARD

When sailing into the wind, if two yachts approach each other on opposite tacks, the boat on the right, Green, is on starboard. The boat on the left, Red, is on port and must give way.

2. WINDWARD KEEPS CLEAR OF LEEWARD

Under the rules Red may luff Green because Red is leeward or downward of Green. For this rule to apply both yachts must be on the same tack.

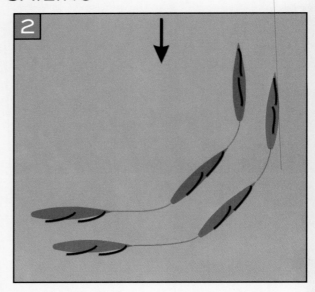

Both *USA-23* and *ITA-25* are on starboard tack with *USA-23* trailing. In this position *USA-23* can choose to control either side of *ITA-25* as it can choose to swing its bow to windward (in this case the right side) or to leeward of *ITA-25*.

THE START

Tactically, the start involves aggressive use of the rules and practised offensive and defensive strategies. Crews will employ a philosophy similar to a fighter pilot trying to win a dogfight against an enemy aircraft as they use the rules to jostle, manoeuvre and establish position. Winning the start can be the deciding factor in 70 percent of all match races.

Yachts must enter the starting area from opposite ends of the starting line 5 minutes before the starting signal. One yacht enters from the starboard side and the other enters from the port side. If either yacht fails to enter the pre-start area within 2 minutes it will be penalised. This rule encourages the boats to meet and engage in pre-start manoeuvring, at least four minutes before the start of the race.

For a helmsman, the start is undoubtedly one of the most tense situations during the entire race. Both yachts, each weighing as much as 25 tons, converge with each other on a collision course. In the strong winds expected in Auckland, these big America's Cup yachts of more than 75 feet are overpowered and extremely difficult to handle. Originally designed for San Diego wind conditions averaging 10 knots, they will face a different proposition in Auckland where they may race in 25 knots.

The sheer momentum of each yacht causes a delay when either yacht manoeuvres. A starboard tack yacht has full rights over a port tack yacht [diagram 1], however the starboard tack yacht cannot do a late turn if, as a result of this turn, the port tack yacht is then unable to keep clear. Therefore, a port tack yacht will try to turn away from a starboard tacker early enough to avoid a collision, but late enough so that the small distance between the yachts will prevent the starboard tacker from altering its course to match that of port. Performed correctly, the port tack yacht may escape the control of a starboard tacker [diagrams 3 and 4].

When yachts are on the same tack, much of the early pre-start advantage is gained by establishing a position astern, or to the right, of the opponent. A following yacht can effectively prevent a yacht in front from turning because a yacht that is changing tacks (turning) has no rights under the rules. Hence a trailing yacht can force an opponent to sail away from the favourable position [diagram 5 and photo p. 159].

To guard against this situation, when both yachts first engage they will often circle each

---

3. LIMITATION ON STARBOARD ALTERING COURSE

Red on port tack tries to keep clear of Green on starboard. Green must give Red an option to escape. Once the boats get very close, Green cannot alter its course unless Red is able to react and still keep clear. In this case Green cannot alter course and Red has escaped the control of Green. The key question umpires ask is whether Red was able to keep clear.

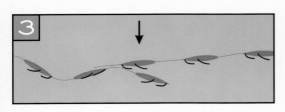

4. LIMITATION ON STARBOARD ALTERING COURSE

Red on port turns to avoid Green on starboard. If Red turns too early, Green will have enough space to turn and aim at Red. Red will again have to keep clear in this case, being forced to tack. Green now controls the right side of the pre-start.

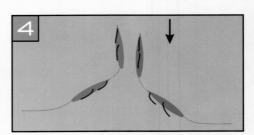

5. CONTROLLING FROM ASTERN

Red can match any course change by Green. Under the rules, Green cannot tack or gybe without fouling Red for two reasons. The rules say Green cannot tack or gybe in Red's water. Also, if Green did tack, or gybe, it would become a port tack yacht that has to give way to Red. Red is therefore controlling Green.

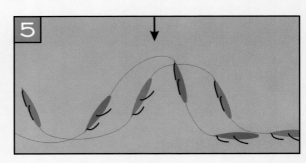

other. When initially circling, neither boat has control over the other [photo A]. However, if one boat is able to circle slightly faster than the other, it will eventually gain the controlling position behind [photo B]. When one yacht begins to lose position, a classic counter-move is to head for the spectator fleet where the lead boat can circle around a spectator vessel without the trailing boat being able to cut inside and block the turn [photos C and D].

On the final approach to the starting line, calculating the distance to the starting line versus the time remaining is the key question. Ideally the yacht will cross the line just after the starting signal. Judging the approach is made more demanding by the changing wind conditions with the boat accelerating, decelerating and changing direction as the wind gusts affect a yacht's performance.

With 25 tons of momentum, a yacht reaching the line too early may find it difficult to slow down enough to avoid crossing early and yet still achieve maximum speed at the starting signal. On the other hand, neither yacht can afford to be late!

6. THE POWER OF A CIRCLING ADVANTAGE

Red, having gained in the circles, tacks close astern of Green. Green must gybe in order to prevent Red setting up in a position close behind. As Green gybes, Red is able to build speed, separating to the right side of Green.

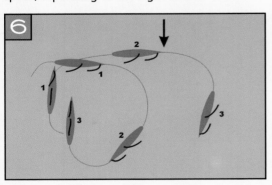

7. CIRCLING CONTINUED

Red now has created enough room to gybe and aim at Green. Green, on port, is forced to tack and Red now controls the right side of the pre-start.

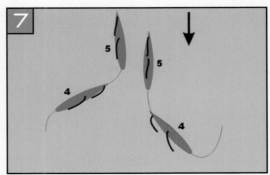

8. EFFECT OF STARTING LINE BIAS

If the wind is not perpendicular to the starting line, it will favour one boat. In this case the wind veers to the right favouring the Red boat, even if Green crosses the starting line first.

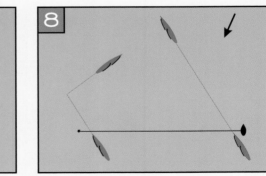

THE FIRST (UPWIND) LEG

After the start the yachts will race into the wind towards a mark that is 3.275 nautical miles away. This leg is often referred to as "the first beat". The wind and current are never constant and will shift during the leg favouring a certain course. On the course area in Auckland the current can be as strong as 2 knots and the wind could shift between 10 and 40 degrees during a single upwind leg. This puts pressure on the tactician who is responsible for reading the wind and currents, as well as predicting what the opponent will do and when they will do it. The tactician then relays that information to the helmsman.

If either boat has gained an advantage at the start, it can choose the favoured tack and will often force the opponent onto the less-favoured course. "Covering" an opponent is one of the most common tactics in match racing, where the leading boat is positioned so that the disturbed wind from its own sails falls onto the opponent's yacht. The trailing yacht is forced to tack in the opposite direction to escape the disturbed wind. If this tack is unfavourable because of a wind shift the loss in distance can be very significant [diagram 9].

A "tight cover" is when a lead boat matches a trailing boat tack for tack, blanketing the wind continuously. The lead crew will usually adopt this tactic if it feels it has an advantage tacking or is uncertain as to which tack is favoured [diagram 10]. The trailing yacht may try everything to break such a cover including "false tacks" when the yacht performs only half the tack and then returns to the original course. The objective is to trick the opponent into going through with the complete tack, thereby gaining "clear air" as the two yachts separate in different directions. The fitness and power of the crew are measured by their performance in the tacks as they furiously work to overcome the power of the sails and outlast the opposition crew.

NZL-38 tacks to cover Nippon. Nippon is forced to tack away to avoid the slowing effects of disturbed wind.

In race four of the 1987 America's Cup challenger series, New Zealand's *KZ-7*, with Chris Dickson at the helm, tacked more than 100 times, tight covering *Stars & Stripes* skippered by Dennis Conner. Although *Stars & Stripes* was the faster boat, *KZ-7* won that race principally because it employed the tight covering tactic.

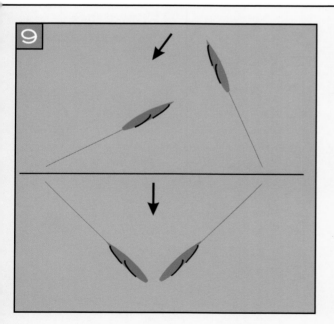

9. THE EFFECT OF WINDSHIFTS
Red and Green are initially even but on opposite tacks. The wind veers right meaning the boat on the right will gain.

10. TIGHT COVERING
Red is tight covering Green. Green will be feeling disturbed wind from Red's influence and will be losing speed.

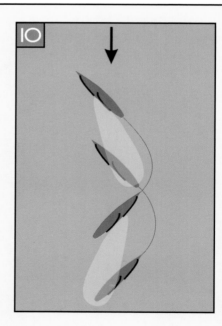

Choosing the correct tack after the start is often predetermined by weather forecasts or a current difference that implies one side of the course will be favoured. The skill of the tactician in reading the wind on the water is vital. The appearance of the water's surface indicates the strength and direction of the approaching wind and can indicate the optimum course much the same as plotting a route using a road map. Occasionally, a crew member will go up the mast to get a better view of the changing conditions. Navigators also record the wind history and current strength on computers that can help to predict the likely wind and current effects.

Starting with the correct sail combination is also a key factor. Sails are designed to have an optimum depth for a particular wind and sea condition. If these conditions change, the crews may consider changing a sail during the leg. Tacticians will balance the gain in performance after a sail change is made with the positional losses that may occur during the change.

There is almost always an opportunity to make gains at the first rounding mark. One of the key decisions in a close race is whether to approach the mark on port or starboard tack. Generally, the starboard tack yacht has more control but the yacht on port can make retaining the lead difficult [diagrams 11 and 12]. Tacticians and navigators work hard to establish the correct line on which to approach or "lay" the mark, called the "layline". Of course in shifting conditions, this approach is constantly changing. If the layline is judged incorrectly, the yacht may be forced to perform two extra tacks, slowing its progress considerably. A slight loss in speed at this point of the race can be very expensive as, after rounding the mark and while the spinnaker is being set, a further speed loss will occur. Once a 25-ton yacht is slowed, it can take more than 45 seconds to accelerate back to the previous speed.

In the America's Cup, all marks are rounded to starboard (or clockwise). The trailing yacht can be positioned to force the leading yacht to perform an extra tack in order to protect its starboard tack rights. The yacht ahead may still hold the lead, but it will have lost some distance and perhaps the controlling position for the following downwind leg.

The red boat on starboard tack has rights over the white boat on port tack. The umpires follow close behind to observe any alterations of course and rule infractions.

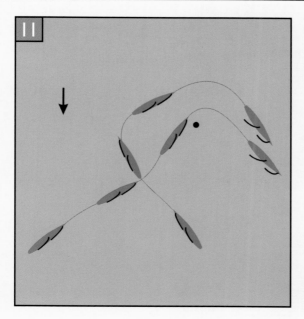

11. EXAMPLE OF PORT TACK ADVANTAGE AT THE TOP MARK
Red on port dips Green's stern very close. Green is forced to sail past Red, because under the rules, Green cannot tack in Red's water. Green therefore sails extra distance, past the layline, and loses the lead.
NB. Green cannot tack before meeting Red because it would not lay the mark.

12. EXAMPLE OF STARBOARD TACK ADVANTAGE AT THE TOP MARK
Red cannot dip Green and still lay the mark. Red must give way to Green because Green is on starboard tack. Green retains the lead.

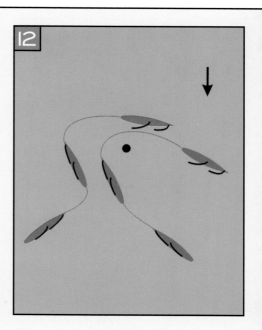

NZL-32 prepares to tack in front of *Stars & Stripes*. Once tacking, *NZL-32* will have no rights until her tack is complete.

THE DOWNWIND LEG

On the downwind leg, called "the run", the trailing boat has the opportunity to attack. Two of the most famous America's Cup races ever sailed are graphic examples of this. In the final and determining seventh race in 1983, *Australia II* overcame a 49-second lead by Dennis Conner on the last leg to become the first non-American yacht to win the America's Cup. In 1995, Conner gained over 4 minutes on the final downwind leg to catch the crew on *Mighty Mary* in the deciding race of the defender trials.

The downwind leg is often payback time for the trailing yacht. When sailing downwind, if the yacht behind is close enough to the opponent to block the wind, it can control or influence the course sailed by the lead yacht. If a yacht can gain an advantage by sailing into stronger winds, the gains downwind are much greater and last longer because the boats are moving at almost the same speed as the wind.

After rounding the windward mark, the decision about which course to choose for the run is critical. Yachts will choose either a bear-away set on port tack or to perform a gybe set onto starboard tack. A gybe set is slower by about half a boat length, but if it results in a position that provides the most favourable breeze, it may be the best option.

Sail choice is critical. The rule allows for either of two different types of downwind spinnakers to be set. One is a symmetrical spinnaker that is set in stronger winds, the other an asymmetric spinnaker or gennaker. While a gennaker is faster in lighter winds than a symmetrical sail, it is also more difficult to gybe. A bad gennaker gybe can be

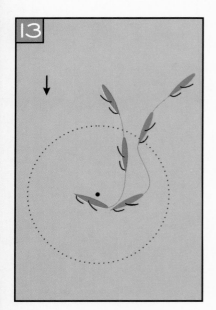

13. ROOM AT THE LEEWARD MARK

Green, on starboard, must give Red, on port, room to round the mark because Red is on the inside when they reach the two-boat-length circle. In this case, rights to room override the rights of starboard tack.

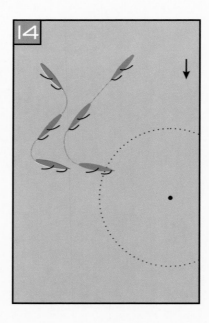

14. ROOM AT THE LEEWARD MARK

Green as starboard tack boat has rights over Red. Red cannot ask for room to round the leeward mark as they have not reached the imaginary two-boat-length circle. Starboard tack rights therefore apply. Green can force Red to sail past the mark and then gybe to lead Red around.

NB: Had Red been able to stay alongside Green after the boats had gybed, Red would have become the inside boat with the right to ask for room.

a race loser and this is always a consideration when choosing between the two sails.

Two positioning options are always debated by the tacticians and strategists as the yachts approach the bottom rounding mark. One is to protect the starboard tack advantage while the other option is to protect the inside position at the mark. The problem is that these two options are in conflict with each other. To retain starboard tack you must stay to the left of an opponent. To gain inside rights you must stay to the right [photo below].

Inside rights come into force only when the yachts are within two boat lengths of the rounding mark. Until that point the boats are governed by the basic racing rules such as port and starboard [diagrams 13, 14 and 15]. However, the advantage of securing the inside position may come into effect much further up the leg. Sometimes yachts will gybe set at the top mark in order to protect inside rights three miles away at the bottom mark! Positioning is critical in both endeavours. In match racing, it is often the case that you will be either rewarded or punished for a decision made 10 minutes earlier during a downwind leg.

The rules for all parts of the race are enforced by on-the-water judges and umpires. Before 1987, yachts used to protest against each other for any perceived infringement and then spend hours after a race debating their case in front of a jury and the penalty was almost always disqualification. Now most of the decisions are instantaneous and although a penalty will cost a yacht approximately six boat lengths in lost distance, the race is not over. The penalised yacht, although disadvantaged, can still come back to win the race. On an upwind leg, the penalty is a gybe. On the downwind leg, a penalised yacht must first lower its spinnaker and then perform a tack before continuing to race.

Some of the more aggressive match-racing skippers have developed moves that may trap an opponent into committing a penalty. Look for these moves during the pre-start manoeuvring and at the rounding marks. If the boats are similar in speed, the difference between winning and losing in the challenger trials and the 2000 America's Cup match may be determined by how well a team know and execute the strategies and tactics of match racing.

15. ROOM AT THE LEEWARD MARK

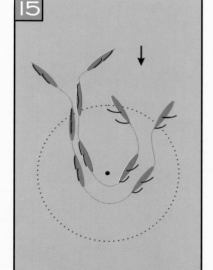

Green must give Red room to round the mark, but after Red has rounded the effect of the "room" rule no longer applies. Green may luff and Red must keep clear. This is a useful move by Green if the left side of the course is favoured, because Red has been forced to the right.

Paul Cayard, at the helm of *Il Moro*, luffs *America³*, helmed by Buddy Melges, on a downwind leg during the 1992 America's Cup match.

CHAPTER 8

America's Cup Technology

Although the America's Cup is a sailboat race, it has often been said that in reality it is a design and technology contest. The winner is determined on the water, but it is what happens on land that often separates the victor from the also-ran. History suggests that the fastest yacht wins and the fastest yacht is usually the fastest design employing the most advanced technology.

It has been that way since the very first challenge when the yacht *America* won the 100 Guinea Cup in 1851. In fact, the men responsible for building *America* did so in an effort to exhibit their nation's proficiency in the technical skills of boat design and boatbuilding. Their yacht, with her sharp bow, wide beam, full stern and low freeboard, was so different from other boats of her type that she was labelled a "radical" schooner. Two steeply raked masts with no topsails and a single jib with no boom completed her appearance of a true racing yacht. When she arrived in England for the race, the Marquis of Anglesey uttered the now famous words, "If she is right, then all of us are wrong". The design was a breakthrough and the yacht was by far the fastest on the 100 Guinea Cup course. This trend has been repeated throughout most of the America's Cup matches that have followed.

Some people believe that the modern regatta would be a fairer contest if it were sailed in identical yachts where the skill of the sailors would be truly measured. Others point out that it is the secrecy, skill, complexity and intrigue surrounding the design that make the Cup so unique and difficult to win.

Conceptually, today's America's Cup may be comparable to Formula One motor racing. Like Formula One, the America's Cup utilises the highest forms of technology in designing and building the most refined racing yachts in the world. While all designers and technicians must adhere to the same formula governing the type of yacht they can produce, they are still given a great deal of creative latitude in which to explore the speed frontier.

Although the racing yachts of today are considerably different from those of early America's Cup competitions, innovation has always been the hallmark of the event. Perhaps the most famous designer and builder in America's Cup history is the legendary American Nathanael Herreshoff. Remembered for his huge yachts that raced in five Cup regattas from 1893 to 1903, "Captain Nat" actually attracted more attention at the time with his succession of small catamarans that tore over the water's surface at speeds upward of 20 miles per hour.

While the multihulls were certainly innovative, it was Herreshoff's creation of *Reliance* that probably stands as his most imaginative work. The largest boat ever to race for the America's Cup, the yacht serves as a clear example of the designer's concept of the exaggerated waterline through the use of extended overhangs forward and aft. The measured waterline length of *Reliance* was a little over 89 feet, but the length overall was close to 144 feet. The result was increased speed as the overhangs translated into increased sailing length.

Herreshoff pushed the design and technology envelope by adding a number of revolutionary notions. *Reliance* carried two steering wheels, a hollow rudder that could be filled with water or pumped dry to correct for weather helm, winches with ball bearings and automatically shifting gears, lightweight steel spars and a topmast that could be lowered into the mainmast for the purpose of saving weight aloft if the topmast was not being used.

As advanced as his design thinking was, it was actually Herreshoff's ideas on boat construction that many historians conclude was his true genius. First employed in building his 1901 Cup defender, the method of "longitudinal construction" was a web of steel frames that connected the keel, hull and deck. The method pioneered by Herreshoff was used in both boat

Nathanael Herreshoff, perhaps the most innovative yacht designer in America's Cup history.

Reliance passing *Blithewold* (1903). Some suggest she was the most scientifically designed sailing vessel ever built.

Enterprise under sail: starboard view (1930).

and airplane construction for the next half century.

One of Herreshoff's contemporaries was George Watson, the designer of Thomas Lipton's second *Shamrock* which raced *Constitution*. The Irish boat was the first to be designed after models were towed in a test tank. This technological process has become a mainstay of America's Cup design ever since.

The 12-metre era from 1958 to 1987 was witness to many technological, design and boatbuilding advances. The first 12-metre defender *Columbia* exhibited the evolutionary reverse transom. The yacht was skippered by Briggs Cunningham who invented the grommeted hole in the mainsail used for trim that is named after him ("the Cunningham eye"). The 1962 challenger *Gretel* was designed by the estimable Alan Payne. He introduced coffee-grinder winches which added speed and efficiency to trimming the jib and tacking the boat. In 1967 the major innovation was the placement of almost all the winches below decks on the defender *Intrepid*. Below-deck winches had been used on both *Reliance* and *Enterprise* (1930), but not to such an extent or in the same configuration.

In 1974, *Courageous*, *Mariner* and *Southern Cross* were the first 12-metre yachts to be built using aluminium, but they weren't the first to be built of that material in the America's Cup. That honour goes to *Defender* in 1895. In 1986, New Zealand's challenger was built using fibreglass. Since then exotic laminates such as carbon-fibre have been used in hull and spar construction.

By 1980, the first of the two-boat programmes was being organised to test and refine various sails, keels and hull changes. One boat was tested against another and as an improvement was found, it would be used to

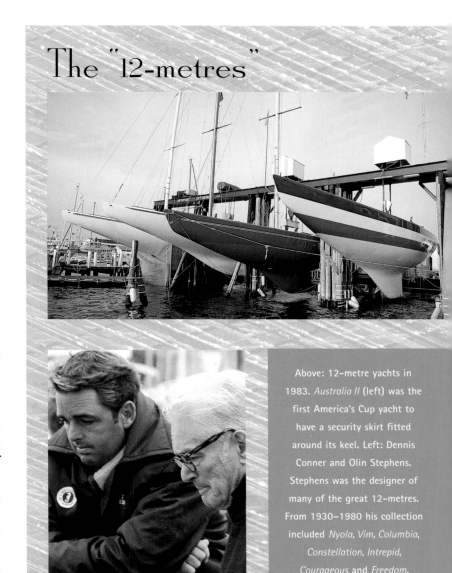

The "12-metres"

Above: 12-metre yachts in 1983. *Australia II* (left) was the first America's Cup yacht to have a security skirt fitted around its keel. Left: Dennis Conner and Olin Stephens. Stephens was the designer of many of the great 12-metres. From 1930–1980 his collection included *Nyala*, *Vim*, *Columbia*, *Constellation*, *Intrepid*, *Courageous* and *Freedom*.

leap-frog the performance of both yachts. Two-boat testing is an expensive and time-consuming method of refining a design. Although it is still used by the larger syndicates today, more confidence is being given to scale model testing.

Much publicity and controversy surrounded the 1983 single boat challenge from Australia, *Australia II*. Alan Bond's syndicate was purported to have used a foreign towing tack to test the widely acclaimed breakthrough wing keel. This was the first challenger to overtake the United States in terms of America's Cup technology – in essence, to beat them at their own game.

In addition, it should be noted that *Australia II* adopted vertically cut upwind sails which better utilised the material properties of the Kevlar sailcloth, a widely used space-age fabric that is both light and extremely stable. In the deciding race, on the final downwind leg, *Australia II* carried a smaller, more settled spinnaker to gain 1 minute 18 seconds passing the American defender *Liberty*. So it is an over-simplification to assume that the wing keel was the only technological advantage *Australia II* enjoyed. *Australia II* beat Dennis Conner's two-boat programme 4-3. Conner was the first American skipper to lose the America's Cup in its then 144-year history.

In 1987 Conner returned, determined to develop a speed edge by using the best American technology available. He adopted the idea of a fully integrated design team.

Conner's team carried out extensive scientific and full-size testing, building three full-size test yachts. The final boat, *Stars & Stripes*, was longer with less sail than any of the opposition. In the strong winds off Fremantle, the yacht enjoyed a significant speed edge to easily out-perform the Australian defender, 4-0.

By 1992, Bill Koch had expanded the team concept to combine some of the top naval architects, marine scientists and engineers in America. He not only hired more scientific expertise than any previous America's Cup syndicate, he also elected to put a scientist rather than a yacht designer at the head of his design group.

Koch was not a renowned sailor by world standards, but he provided a new management style that focused on technology. He stipulated that the yacht should be fast enough so that even he would be able to helm it and win! The team produced *America³* which, with Bill Koch as co-helmsman, easily beat the Italian challenger, *Il Moro di Venezia*, 4-1.

In 1995, it was widely accepted that it would be very difficult to improve on Bill Koch's design effort. But on the other side of the world, the Kiwis had assembled a formidable team who set out to challenge the level achieved by Koch. Many were surprised by the speed advantage that was subsequently attained. The New Zealand boat *Black Magic* became only the second non-American yacht to win the America's Cup, sweeping the defender 5-0. It was later observed that had *Black Magic* raced *America³*, the New Zealand boat might have won by more than five minutes!

All of the syndicates competing in the 1999/2000 Cup will adopt a scientific approach and initially structure themselves as large research programmes. To make the breakthroughs that all Cup syndicates seek, today's yacht designer has a number of tools at his disposal which until recently were non existent. Chief among these is the personal computer, which accomplishes a variety of tasks essential to design. As the computer has become more powerful and more versatile, it seems it is being used for everything from drawing hull lines to analysing competitors' shapes to acquiring real-time data while sailing. What used to be done by hand over a period of months in the days of such America's Cup boats as *Ranger* (1937), *Columbia* (1958), *Constellation* (1964), *Intrepid* (1967), and even *Courageous* in 1974, now has been reduced to a matter of hours as CAD-CAM (Computer Assisted Design, Computer Assisted Manufacturing) programs attack a myriad of problems.

Other time-saving methods and use of scientific disciplines have made the design process more efficient. Development in scale modelling, computer codes, engineering, aerodynamics and hydrodynamics has enabled designers to gain a greater understanding of the environmental factors and the materials that are responsible for producing additional boatspeed.

Previous yachts and components are rapidly outdated and become little more than test platforms to perform tests and confirm new concepts. With modern technology, more candidate designs can be considered over a shorter time span and at less cost. It may therefore not be unrealistic to expect significant improvements by the time the America's Cup final commences in February 2000. Consideration should also be given to the change in venue. The light conditions of San Diego have been replaced with the unpredictable and sometimes rugged conditions in Auckland.

An advantage of only a few seconds can mean the difference between gaining the controlling position or being controlled. Most of the sailing teams are capable of capitalising on such a position and force the opposition onto the unfavoured tack. A small difference in boatspeed rapidly increases to minutes in predictable wind conditions.

So let us consider some of the choices that were contemplated when designing an America's Cup yacht for Auckland conditions. The three basic design parameters contained in the IACC rule are length (measured 200mm above the waterline), sail area and weight (or displacement).

Carnage in San Diego. Three broken masts, one on *Stars & Stripes* (above), one on *Defi France* (left) and the other on *Nippon* (below left). Auckland's extreme conditions will put an even greater emphasis on structural design. Below: In New Zealand conditions, broken sails will be a factor.

"Wave Drag". The 12-metres were heavy with short keels. In stronger winds, they produced a large wave trough, which was a large component of the hull drag.

The longer a yacht, the faster it will sail, particularly at high speeds when the yacht's own wake and waves become a large component of the overall drag.

Additional sail area is always fast in light winds and when sailing downwind, except in very light winds or choppy seas where a big spinnaker may become unstable. However, in strong winds when sailing on an upwind leg, too much sail will only increase the drag. In all yachts there is a windspeed above which it is faster to reef or reduce sail area.

Increasing the weight of a yacht increases the amount of water that is displaced. It may therefore be presumed that, generally, a heavier boat will sail slower than a lighter boat. However, in the case of an America's Cup boat, increasing the weight usually means increasing the amount of lead on the bottom of the keel (the bulb). The force provided by the bulb opposes the moments created by the sails. Therefore, with a heavier bulb, more driving force may be utilised from the sails. IACC yachts will usually float longer when weight is added because the rule allows overhanging sterns and bows. Therefore, even if weight were added making the boat displace more water, in certain conditions the additional length and stability may provide more boat speed! Accordingly, the rules restrict the amount of additional weight that can be carried.

Such may have been the case during the defender trials in 1987. *Australia IV* was holed after a collision and began to take on water. Much to the surprise of the crew, *Australia IV* began to sail faster.

It would be trivial to design a faster yacht if there were no rule constraints. Dennis Conner

Four prominent America's Cup yacht designers: Doug Peterson, Mike Drummond, Dr Jerry Milgram and Bruce Nelson.

Team New Zealand meteorologist Bob Rice studies weather data in San Diego.

Dave Hubbard – the designer of the solid wing sail on the 1988 catamaran defence.

showed this in 1988 in a catamaran. Working within the America's Cup rule provides the intrigue and the challenge of who can create the fastest yacht. Designers are faced with the delicate balance of finding the optimum parameters within the limits of the America's Cup rule.

The governing formula is:

$$\frac{L+1.25 \times \sqrt{S} - 9.8 \times \sqrt[3]{DSP}}{0.679} \leq 24.00m$$

L = rated length in metres
S = rated sail area in square metres
DSP = displacement in cubic metres

Before 1992, the America's Cup was raced under a similar rule except the constant was 12 metres. The rated length term in the governing formula is further defined as follows:

$$L = LM \times (1+0.01 \times (LM-21.2)^8) + FP + DP + WP + BP$$

different from many modern race yachts in that it may have significant overhang at one or both ends which adds to the "sailing length" of the yacht. G attempts to make allowance for these features and apply them into the length formula. BP, WP, DP are all zero except when (respectively) the beam exceeds 5.500m, or the weight is not between 16,000-25,000kg, or the draft is greater than 4.000m.

The rule provides for a maximum mast height above the deck of 32.500m and the spinnaker pole length and spinnaker area is related to the choice of the length of the base of the foretriangle (J) (dia.). Apart from construction and material constraints the rule is relatively simple and open.

There are several significant features in the IACC rule that are different from many other modern yacht design rules.

First, the IACC rule contains no measurement of stability. Teams are therefore encouraged to build their yachts as light as possible above the keel in order to gain as much stability as possible. This creates a huge engineering challenge to design a yacht near the minimum strength required to withstand the massive sailing loads applied. Rigging loads can approach 25 tons, and the compression load on the mast more than 50 tons, straining the lightweight carbon-fibre structures. With no restriction on stability, all America's Cup boats use very large bulbs on the bottom of their keel to balance the huge overturning forces created by the sails and mast whilst sailing upwind. These bulbs typically weigh between 16,000kg–20,000kg and are supported on a thin keel strut that is connected to the hull. It is not unusual for these keel struts to deflect more than 100mm under sailing conditions!

The second major difference in the rule is that there is no restriction on minimum beam. All yachts will be designed under the beam limit (without penalty) of 5.500m and the question is how narrow to build the boat? Reducing beam reduces wetted surface, until the yacht becomes almost semi-circular in cross-section. However, reducing beam also reduces stability and the designers will therefore have to relate beam to their choice of optimum wind strength.

Pressure Distribution

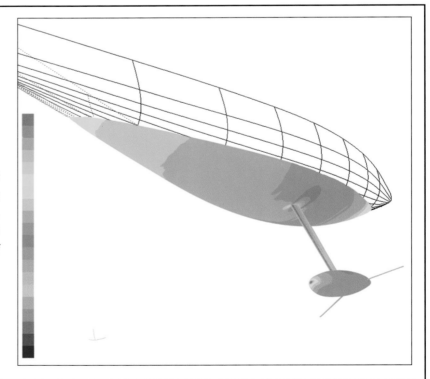

The diagram shows the complete appendage set minus the rudder in a typical upwind sailing condition (with the boat heeled and making leeway). It was calculated using the Fluent Code (with 1.6 million grid points) on an SGI Origin. The areas of highest pressure are shown in red.

Keels

ELLIPTICAL

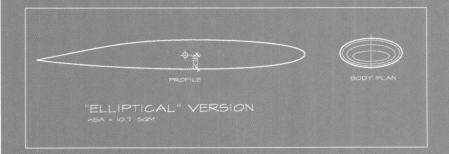

PROFILE   BODY PLAN

"ELLIPTICAL" VERSION
WSA = 10.7 SQM

Keel on *oneAustralia* 1995. It was longer and more squashed than many of the designs seen in San Diego featuring a low vertical centre of gravity but high wetted surface. It was therefore an attempt to improve the yacht's upwind performance while accepting a loss in speed downwind.

SLUMPED

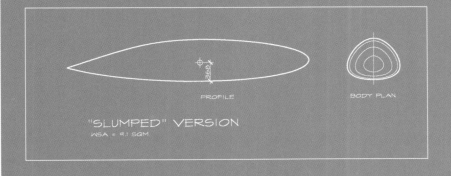

PROFILE   BODY PLAN

"SLUMPED" VERSION
WSA = 9.1 SQM

The keel on *NZL-32* was moderately slumped and featured small wings with a shorter than usual trim tab on the back of the keel fin.

ROUND

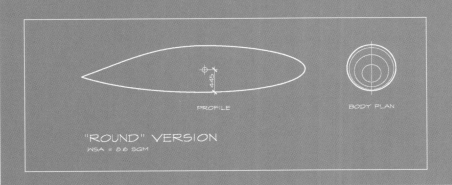

PROFILE   BODY PLAN

"ROUND" VERSION
WSA = 8.6 SQM

Keel on *Stars & Stripes* 1995. It has more rounded sections and is short, therefore having a higher vertical centre of gravity. It is a low wetted surface option which was a desirable feature for the light wind conditions in San Diego. Note the hollows at the bulb/fin intersection which were intended to smooth out the changes in pressure.

Above: The Italian syndicate was the first challenger to start full-scale two-boat testing in Auckland conditions. Below left: In 1995, the French developed a sail plan in which the mainsail was not attached to the mast. They tested the concept using half-scale models, where it was reputed to be fast. Below right: In 1980, Australia adapted a bendy mast, originally developed by the British Victory syndicate, as a way to increase their sail area.

Designers will therefore consider the balance that a wider boat may be faster upwind in stronger winds but slower in lighter winds and when sailing downwind.

The third difference is that hull shape is relatively unrestricted within the basic parameters. Many rules contain measurements of hull shape and make allowances for perceived better shapes. The America's Cup rule is more open although there can be no hollows and there is a volume restriction (girth) at the forward and aft waterline stations. The "no hollows" part of the rule is actually very powerful in preventing the distortions that were present in the 12-metre and IOR design rules. Designers are therefore relatively free to choose their fastest smooth shape within their chosen length and beam.

So the basic rule trade-offs are relatively simple. A longer boat will need either less sail or more weight to measure under the rule. A lighter boat may similarly have less sail or be shorter. A yacht with more sail area will need to be shorter or heavier.

However the specific choice of parameters will be very complicated, and crucial to any team's success in 2000. Auckland will present the most varied conditions ever experienced in America's Cup history. Wind speeds could vary between 8 and 30 knots, possibly all within the span of a single race! Wave conditions are likely to be relatively smooth in a southerly wind direction and yet very rough when the wind swings to the northerly quadrant. Designing for sea conditions may require a totally different treatment for detailing the forward sections of the hull, depending on the decision taken to optimise for smooth or rough water.

In southerly wind conditions, windshifts and oscillations in a breeze ranging between 10-30 degrees will not be uncommon and so will require more tacking and manoeuvring from the yachts. These conflicting natural conditions will no doubt promote a lot of thought and discussion pertaining to the choices of length, beam, bow shape, sail area, weight and structural stiffness required for the "ideal" yacht to race in 2000.

Let us now consider the various design tools used to allow decisions and conclusions to be made on design choices.

Perhaps the first things to quantify are the perceived areas for improvement balanced against the required time and money needed to complete each project. This is an important question that every design team face at the start of their programme. The America's Cup race is a technology race testing which team can create the fastest boat within their financial resources and within the time constraints and measurement deadlines. In the past, many teams have failed by wasting large portions of their design budgets chasing small or unachievable gains, or by simply running out of time. Race dates are fixed and there would be little future in trying to convince your competitors to delay racing until your testing requirements are finalised!

A test matrix is developed listing the various features requiring further testing. Teams usually invest in experience by acquiring the services of top yacht designers, scientists, aerodynamic experts and engineers who can use their knowledge from previous testing to reduce the amount of testing required. In many instances, when a design choice cannot be validated, intuition and experience play a vital role.

Full-size testing is both slow and very expensive. Only a very limited number of tests and options can be performed within the given time frame and the test conditions often involve a complex series of wind conditions and variables. Achieving consistent results is very difficult in controlled laboratory conditions, let alone in the natural environment!

Measuring and separating the individual components is often impractical when testing full size, therefore gaining a true understanding of the reasons for results is often confusing. Full-size testing is often necessary to validate computer codes and scale testing methods. If a design team develop confidence and accuracy in their computational methods by full-size testing, then the chances of obtaining a speed edge using the design codes are significantly enhanced.

The modern design team therefore use a combination of methods to cross-check and confirm test results. These may include several VPPs (velocity prediction programs), water tunnel or towing tank, wind tunnel, engineering programs such as FE (finite element) studies, sail programs and CFD codes (computational fluid dynamics).

The VPP is the central design tool and involves a program developed for a computer that is based on a series of mathematical formulae and imperial measurements. A VPP balances the sail forces (forward and side) with the lift and drag of the hull and appendages at various windspeeds and sailing angles. A VPP will predict the optimum speeds that various candidate test yachts might achieve in a variety of wind and sea conditions. The VPP utilises most of the relevant speed-related factors including length, beam, hull stiffness, hull shape, stability, wetted surface area, sail area, rig windage, crew weight and sea conditions to output each prediction. Some of these factors are relatively simple to predict but others such as sea conditions are more difficult to validate because of the randomness of the wave spectrum.

The sail forces are also very difficult to predict and measure. This is also not made any easier by the variation and turbulence of the wind spectrum both horizontally and vertically.

In 1992, *America³* built a half-scale yacht that was fitted with strain gauges to isolate the sail forces under various sailing conditions. The primary objective was to validate and refine their VPP and CFD sail codes.

The towing tank is used to measure the differences in candidate hulls and appendages. Scale models are towed from a carriageway down a large pool (often 200m in length). The forces are measured, scaled to full size, averaged and corrected before the data is applied to a VPP where the hull forces are combined with the sail forces. The towing tank is also used to isolate and validate various features that are incorporated into a VPP.

The interpretation of the data is a key skill because many of the model forces scale differently. Frictional drag forces scale differently from pressure drag which also scales differently from wave drag. Many suggest that the accuracy is improved when large-scale models are used. *America³* used half-scale models in 1992 while Team New Zealand used quarter-scale models in 1995. Most agree that models less than one-ninth scale are too small to achieve the required accuracy.

The wind tunnel is generally used for appendage work and sail measurements. High-speed tunnels can generate similar conditions for the candidate model as experienced full-size. Air moving at 100 knots is equivalent to water moving at 1.5 knots. It is ideal to operate the tunnel at similar Reynolds' numbers where the wake conditions will be a true representation of reality.

One of the complicated factors when modelling sailing vessels is that you must deal with the boundary between water and air. Even though the appendages are attached below the water surface, they are still close enough to contribute to the surface waves. The forward and side forces on a yacht's hull and keel combine to produce a complex series of waves and wave troughs, the extent of which provides a significant component of the overall drag [photo pp. 176-7].

Team New Zealand also utilised a wind tunnel to measure sail forces in 1995. One-ninth scale models were used to refine general concepts in sail shape and size. The allowable design space for spinnakers alone is very broad with the rule concentrating on sail areas only. Such things as aspect ratios and shapes were tested using the wind tunnel and then in some cases validated full size. This reduced the amount of full-size sail testing and increased the practical limit for the design matrix with eventually more than 120 spinnaker models being tested.

There is no doubt that technology will play a large part in the outcome of the America's Cup in 2000. The biggest budget will not necessarily win. As has been proven through history, the team which develop the fastest boat will probably win. ⚓

Scale Testing Methods

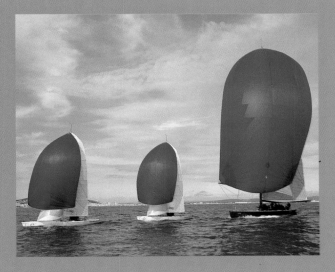

Above: Storage of candidate models for future testing. Above right: The half-scale models the French used for testing. Below: The towing tank showing the hull attached to the carriageway. Water conditions must be perfectly stable before each test run is performed. Some of the modern hulls have also been tested in towing tanks that can generate waves. Bottom left: Team New Zealand sail designer Michael Eckart checks the forces generated from the University of Auckland twisted flow wind tunnel. Bottom right: Flow visualisation using smoke traces.

Course Chart

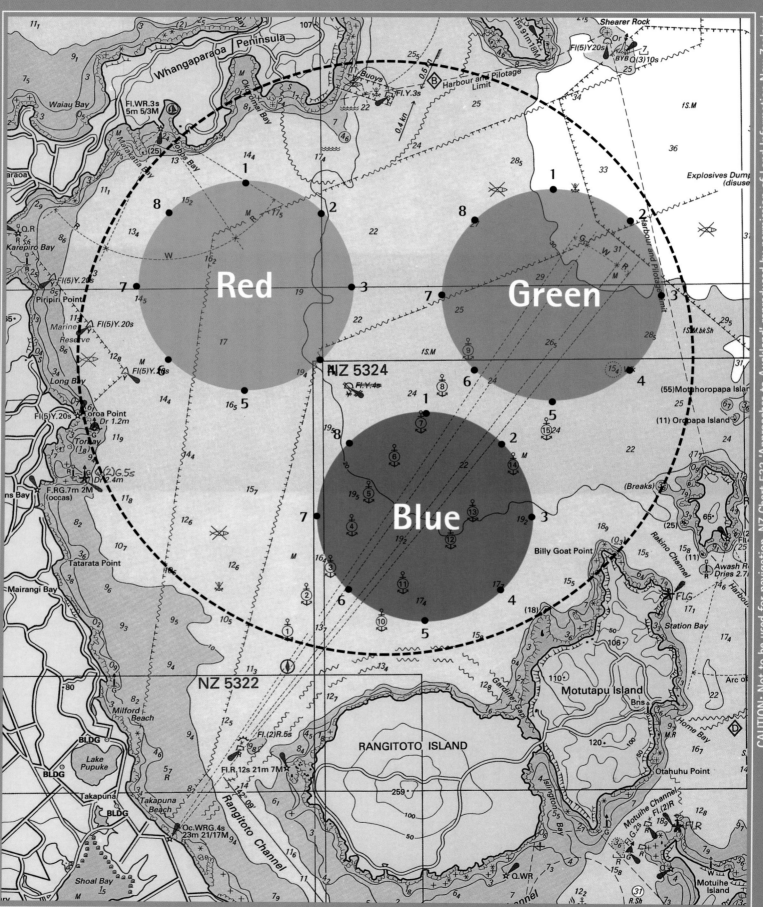

The Red, Green and Blue areas are for the challengers' round robins and defender's racing.
The America's Cup match races will use all water that is free from headlands inside the dotted circle.

SCHEDULE OF RACES

LOUIS VUITTON CUP

Round Robin One

One point per win

18 – 23 October 1999
Six Racing Days

24 October – 5 November 1999
Reserve Days

Round Robin Two

Four points per win

6 – 16 November 1999
Eleven Racing Days

17 – 26 November 1999
Reserve Days

Round Robin Three

Nine points per win

2 – 12 December 1999
Eleven Racing Days

13 – 24 December 1999
Reserve Days

Semi-Finals

The top six points winners from the Round Robins advance to the Semi-Finals

2 – 11 January 2000
Ten Racing Days

12 – 19 January 2000
Reserve Days

Finals

The two top points winners from the Semi-Finals advance to the best-of-nine Finals

25 – 27 January 2000
Races 1-3

2 – 4 February 2000
Races 7-9

29 – 31 January 2000
Races 4-6

5 – 13 February 2000
Reserve Days

AMERICA'S CUP

Best-of-Nine Series

19 February 2000
Race 1

24 February 2000
Race 4

29 February 2000
Race 7

20 February 2000
Race 2

26 February 2000
Race 5

2 March 2000
Race 8

22 February 2000
Race 3

27 February 2000
Race 6

4 March 2000
Race 9

5, 7, 9 March 2000
Reserve Days

Crew Positions

a Bowman

The bowman connects the sheets and halyards to the sails before they are changed. When a spinnaker is changed, the bowman must connect the new sail to the outside end of the spinnaker pole. The bowman is usually sent aloft when a problem on the mast arises. During the pre-start, the bowman uses hand signals to convey positioning information about the start line to the helmsman.

b Midbow

Like the bowman, the midbow is a very physical position. The midbowman works with the bowman and the mastman to perform all sail changes. He also packs the sails below decks so they can be used again if required. Sails gain weight when they are wet, making the handling and packing work difficult. But since the midbowman also shares grinding duties, the faster the sails are packed, the quicker the new sails can be trimmed.

c Mastman

The mastman uses his weight to hoist the sails, often jumping off the deck to pull on the halyards while the pitman takes up the slack in the line. In a hoist, the mastman and a grinder will work together, jumping alternately to set the sail as quickly as possible. In a jibe, the mastman works with the midbowman to position the spinnaker pole.

d Pitman

The pitman generally runs the forward half of the yacht, controlling and communicating all the halyards and sail changes that must be performed during the course of the race. When sails are not being changed, the pitman becomes a grinder so the position benefits from someone who has size and strength.

e Grinders

This job requires weight, strength and fitness as well as a knowledge of trim so that the grinder can react instantly. America's Cup yachts are not allowed to have electric winches or pumps, so most tasks are performed manually. Aside from weight and strength, speed and endurance are critical to this position.

f Genoa/Spinnaker trimmers

Usually there are at least two genoa/spinnaker trimmers on an America's Cup yacht. They work with the helmsman and mainsail trimmer to optimize the yacht's performance. Changing genoas and spinnakers during changes in conditions is often an important strategic move during competition and sail selection is the responsibility of the trimmers.

g Running backstay trimmers

The running backstays are the ropes that provide tension on the headstays when sailing upwind and also prevent the mast from falling over the bow when sailing downwind. The load on the headstay can be as much as 25 tons and each time the yacht changes tacks, tension must be applied by the new runner. The runner also has a huge influence on the shape of the genoa.

h Tactician

The tactician uses the technical information provided by the navigator and weather forecasters, together with his own observation of the wind and wave conditions, to ascertain the best course for the yacht to sail. The tactician must plan the strategy using the wind shifts and other local effects to out-manoeuvre the opponent, much like in a game of chess. Forecasting the wind is an inexact science, so the tactician must balance the risks and rewards for a given race situation before making his recommendation to the helmsman.

i Skipper/Helmsman

The tactician and navigator feed strategic and tactical information which the helmsman uses to position the boat. The helmsman steers the boat and communicates the "feel" of the boat to the sail trimmers to obtain optimum speed. In close boat-on-boat situations and pre-start positioning, the helmsman decides the tactics.

j Mainsail trimmer

Most mainsails will measure between 200 and 225 square metres, obviously contributing significantly to the performance of the boat. The mainsail trimmer therefore works with the mainsail trimmer to determine the speed of the yacht and must work closely with the helmsman, genoa trimmers and tacticians to change the boat's performance for a given situation.

k Traveller trimmer

The traveller is what determines the angle of the main boom to the wind when sailing into the wind. The traveller trimmer therefore works with the mainsail trimmer to determine the correct mainsail shape. In the pre-start, during mark roundings, and when sailing downwind, the traveller trimmer becomes a mainsail grinder.

l Navigator

The navigator uses on-board computers and global positioning systems to pass on accurate information to the tacticians, helmsman and sail trimmers. That information may include the precise position of the boat on the race course, the yacht's relative performance versus the opponent's boat, and wind trends occurring on the course.

ROLL OF HONOUR

YEAR	YACHT	YACHT CLUB	NATION	SKIPPER	DESIGNER	LOCATION	SCORE
1851	Winner: America Rival: Fleet of 15 British yachts	New York Yacht Club	USA	C. Brown	George Steers	Cowes, GB	1-0
1870	Winner: Magic Rival: Cambria	New York Yacht Club Royal Thames	USA Great Britain	A. Cornstock J. Tannock	R. S. Loper M. Ratsey	New York, USA	1-0
1871	Winner: Columbia/Sappho Rival: Livonia	New York Yacht Club Royal Harwich	USA Great Britain	N. Cornstock/S. Greenwood J. R. Woods	J. Van Deusen/D. Kerby M. Ratsey	New York, USA	4-1
1876	Winner: Madeleine Rival: Countess of Dufferin	New York Yacht Club Royal Canadian	USA Canada	J. Williams J. E. Ellsworth	G. A. Smith A. Cuthbert	New York, USA	2-0
1881	Winner: Mischief Rival: Atalanta	New York Yacht Club Bay of Quinte	USA Canada	N. Clock J. E. Ellsworth	A. Cary Smith A. Cuthbert	New York, USA	2-0
1885	Winner: Puritan Rival: Genesta	New York Yacht Club Royal Yacht Squadron	USA Great Britain	A. J. Crocker J. Carter	Edward Burgess J. Beavor-Webb	New York, USA	2-0
1886	Winner: Mayflower Rival: Galatea	New York Yacht Club Royal Northern	USA Great Britain	M. Stone J. Carter	Edward Burgess J. Beavor-Webb	New York, USA	2-0
1887	Winner: Volunteer Rival: Thistle	New York Yacht Club Royal Clyde	USA Great Britain	H. C. Haff J. Barr	Edward Burgess George Watson	New York, USA	2-0
1893	Winner: Vigilant Rival: Valkyrie II	New York Yacht Club Royal Yacht Squadron	USA Great Britain	W. Hansen W. Cranfield	N. Herreshoff George Watson	New York, USA	3-0
1895	Winner: Defender Rival: Valkyrie III	New York Yacht Club Royal Yacht Squadron	USA Great Britain	H. C. Haff W. Cranfield	N. Herreshoff George Watson	New York, USA	3-0
1899	Winner: Columbia Rival: Shamrock I	New York Yacht Club Royal Ulster	USA Northern Ireland	C. Barr A. Hogarth	N. Herreshoff William Fife Jr.	New York, USA	3-0
1901	Winner: Columbia Rival: Shamrock II	New York Yacht Club Royal Ulster	USA Northern Ireland	C. Barr E. A. Sycamore	N. Herreshoff George Watson	New York, USA	3-0
1903	Winner: Reliance Rival: Shamrock III	New York Yacht Club Royal Ulster	USA Northern Ireland	C. Barr R. Wringe	N. Herreshoff William Fife Jr.	New York, USA	3-0
1920	Winner: Resolute Rival: Shamrock IV	New York Yacht Club Royal Ulster	USA Northern Ireland	C. F. Adams W. Burton	N. Herreshoff Charles E. Nicholson	New York, USA	3-2
1930	Winner: Enterprise Rival: Shamrock V	New York Yacht Club Royal Ulster	USA Northern Ireland	H. Vanderbilt N. Heard	Starling Burgess Charles E. Nicholson	Newport, USA	4-0
1934	Winner: Rainbow Rival: Endeavour	New York Yacht Club Royal Yacht Squadron	USA Great Britain	H. Vanderbilt T. O. M. Sopwith	Starling Burgess Charles E. Nicholson	Newport, USA	4-2
1937	Winner: Ranger Rival: Endeavour II	New York Yacht Club Royal Yacht Squadron	USA Great Britain	H. Vanderbilt T. O. M. Sopwith	S. Burgess/O. Stephens Charles E. Nicholson	Newport, USA	4-0
1958	Winner: Columbia Rival: Sceptre	New York Yacht Club Royal Yacht Squadron	USA Great Britain	B. Cunningham G. Mann	Olin Stephens David Boyd	Newport, USA	4-0
1962	Winner: Weatherly Rival: Gretel	New York Yacht Club Royal Sydney Yacht Squadron	USA Australia	B. Mosbacher J. Sturrock	Phil Rhodes Alan Payne	Newport, USA	4-1
1964	Winner: Constellation Rival: Sovereign	New York Yacht Club Royal Thames	USA Great Britain	R. Bavier/E. Ridder P. Scott	Olin Stephens David Boyd	Newport, USA	4-0
1967	Winner: Intrepid Rival: Dame Pattie	New York Yacht Club Royal Sydney Yacht Squadron	USA Australia	B. Mosbacher J. Sturrock	Olin Stephens Warwick Hood	Newport, USA	4-0
1970	Winner: Intrepid Rival: Gretel II	New York Yacht Club Royal Sydney Yacht Squadron	USA Australia	B. Ficker J. Hardy	O. Stephens/B. Chance Alan Payne	Newport, USA	4-1
1974	Winner: Courageous Rival: Southern Cross	New York Yacht Club Royal Perth Yacht Club	USA Australia	R. Bavier J. Cuneo	Olin Stephens Bob Miller (Ben Lexcen)	Newport, USA	4-0
1977	Winner: Courageous Rival: Australia	New York Yacht Club Sun City	USA Australia	T. Turner N. Robins	Sparkman/Stephens Ben Lexcen/Johan Valentijn	Newport, USA	4-0
1980	Winner: Freedom Rival: Australia	New York Yacht Club Royal Perth Yacht Club	USA Australia	D. Conner J. Hardy	Sparkman/Stephens Ben Lexcen/Johan Valentijn	Newport, USA	4-1
1983	Winner: Australia II Rival: Liberty	Royal Perth Yacht Club New York Yacht Club	Australia USA	J. Bertrand D. Conner	Ben Lexcen Johan Valentijn	Newport, USA	4-3
1987	Winner: Stars & Stripes Rival: Kookaburra III	San Diego Yacht Club Royal Perth Yacht Club	USA Australia	D. Conner I. Murray	Design team Design team led by I. Murray	Perth, Australia	4-0
1988	Winner: Stars & Stripes Rival: New Zealand	San Diego Yacht Club Mercury Bay Boating Club	USA New Zealand	D. Conner D. Barnes	Design team Design team led by B. Farr	San Diego, USA	3-0
1992	Winner: America[3] Rival: Il Moro di Venezia	San Diego Yacht Club Compagnia della Vela	USA Italy	B. Koch P. Cayard	Design team Design team	San Diego, USA	4-1
1995	Winner: Black Magic Rival: Young America	Royal NZ Yacht Squadron New York Yacht Club	New Zealand USA	Russell Coutts D. Conner	Design team Design team	San Diego, USA	5-0

INDEX

GLOSSARY

Back   A counter-clockwise wind shift.

Backstays   Adjustable lines that support the rig from the stern to the top section of the mast.

Beam   The width of the boat at its widest point.

Beat   See "Upwind".

Bear Away Set   To hoist and set a spinnaker without gybing.

Cockpit   Lower and aft portion of the deck where most of the crew operate.

Dipping/Dip/Duck   To pass astern of another yacht.

Downwind   Sailing a course with the wind. Yachts gybe to change tack when sailing downwind.

Foot   The bottom of a sail.

Foredeck   Deck in front of the mast.

Forestay   Fixed length rod-stay attached below the top of the mast to the bow, which supports the jib luff.

Gennaker   An asymmetric spinnaker used in lighter breezes when sailing downwind.

Gybe Set   To hoist a spinnaker after/as the gybe is being completed.

Gybing   When the boat changes direction downwind to take the wind on the other side of the boat.

Halyard   A rope used to hoist and lower the sails.

Head   The top of the sail.

Head to Wind   When the bow points directly at the wind and the sails will be flapping.

Headsails   The sails that are attached to the forestay. These act like the boat's gears and are changed up and down in size and weight depending on wind speed. They are numbered according to their size/weight. The lighter the wind, the bigger and deeper the sail.

Leach   The back of the sail.

Leeward   Downwind side of the yacht.

Luff   The front of the sail.

Layline   An imaginary straight line tracing the course along which a yacht can fetch a mark, without tacking or gybing while sailing at its optimum speed.

Main Boom   Horizontal spar that holds the foot of the mainsail.

Mainsail   The large sail flown from the trailing (back) edge of the mast.

Mast   Vertical spar that holds up the sails and supports the mainsail luff. Also known as the "rig".

Port   The left side of the boat as you face forward.

Port Tack   Sailing with the wind coming from the port side of the boat.

Rail   Edge of the deck where the crew sit, with their legs over the side in stronger winds.

Reach   To sail with the wind approximately side on to the yacht.

Run   Legs 2, 4 and 6 are downwind legs or "runs".

Sheets   The ropes used to trim sails.

Sidestays   These rigid rod-stays support the rig sideways. Also known as the ìshroudsî.

Spinnaker   This is the big balloon-like sail used when sailing downwind. Itís also known as a "kite" or "chute".

Starboard   The right side of the boat as you face forward.

Starboard Tack   Sailing with the wind coming from the starboard side of the boat.

Start/Finish Line   A line sighted between a mast on the committee boat and a buoy, separated by approximately 200 metres.

Tacking   This is when the yacht changes direction and takes the wind on the other side of the boat as it ìtacksî into the wind. As the yacht passes through ìhead to windî the sails will flap until the yacht has turned far enough (approximately 40º) away from the true wind direction. The boat will sail a series of zig-zags as it ìtacksî towards an upwind mark.

Telltails   These are pieces of thread attached to strategic points of the sails to indicate windflow.

Upwind   Sailing a course approximately 40º to the true wind direction. Legs 1, 3 and 5 are beats. Yachts ìtackî into the wind.

Veer   A clockwise wind shift.

Velocity Made Good (VMG)   The speed a yacht is making relative to the direction of the wind. When sailing upwind the best VMG is between 50º – 30º angle to the wind. When sailing downwind, the best VMG is (135º – 170º) angle to the wind.

Windward   Upwind side of the yacht.